Scarecrow Film Score Guides
Series Editor: Kate Daubney

Danny Elfman's
Batman

A Film Score Guide

Janet K. Halfyard

Scarecrow Film Score Guides, No. 2

The Scarecrow Press, Inc.
Lanham, Maryland • Toronto • Oxford
2004

781.54
E39B

SCARECROW PRESS, INC.

Published in the United States of America
by Scarecrow Press, Inc.
A wholly owned subsidary of
The Rowman & Littlefield Publishing Group, Inc.
4501 Forbes Boulevard, Suite 200, Lanham, Maryland 20706
www.scarecrowpress.com

PO Box 317
Oxford
OX2 9RU, UK

British Library Cataloguing in Publication Information Available

Library of Congress Cataloging-in-Publication Data

Halfyard, Janet K., 1966–
  Danny Elfman's Batman : a film score guide / Janet K. Halfyard.
    p. cm. — (Scarecrow film score guides ; no. 2)
  Includes bibliographical references (p.   ) and index.
  ISBN 0-8108-5126-1 (pbk. : alk. paper)
  1. Elfman, Danny. Batman. I. Title. II. Series.
ML410.E396H35 2004
781.5'42—dc22

                                        2004006852

To my parents

Contents

Editor's Foreword

This is the second volume in the new Scarecrow series of Film Score Guides (formerly published by Greenwood), a set of books dedicated to drawing together the variety of different analytical practices and ideological approaches in film musicology for the study of individual scores. Much value has been drawn from case studies of film scoring practice in other film music texts, but these guides offer a substantial, wide-ranging, and comprehensive study of a single score. Subjects are chosen for the series on the basis that they have become and are widely recognized as a benchmark for the way in which film music is composed and experienced. A guide explores the context of a score's composition through its place in the career of the composer and its relationship to the techniques of the composer. The context of the score in narrative and production terms is also considered, and readings of the film as a whole are discussed in order to situate in their filmic context the musical analyses that conclude the guide. Furthermore, although these guides focus on the score as written text—bringing forward often previously unknown details about the process of composition as they are manifested in the manuscript—analysis also includes exploration of the music as an aural text, for this is the first and, for most audiences, the only way in which they will experience the music of the film.

This volume on *Batman* marks the first in-depth academic study of a score by Danny Elfman, a composer whose work has caused more debate than that of many of his contemporaries. It is a mark of the complex position that film music occupies in the critical consciousness of musicology in general, that so much of this debate has focused on Elfman's technical approach. Questions about the seriousness or validity of the process through which he composes his scores have generated diverse critical viewpoints in the appreciation of his music within and without its filmic context. This is a deliberation that shows both how much and how little film musicology has evolved from early discussions of the scores of the Golden Age composers, such as Erich Korngold and Max Steiner. The original parameters for legitimizing their work often centered on their perceived 'concert hall' pedigree, and these parameters framed the appreciation of what their music brought to film. Elfman's eclectic rock background to his recognizable orchestral and vocal film music idiom could not contrast more, and yet it has generated a conflict in the routine of critical evaluation; we still insist on measuring quality in relation to stylistic origin, but are troubled when we must accommodate successful film music born of unorthodox parents. This is a conflict that Dr. Halfyard explores from a number of different angles, and her thorough and all-encompassing analysis in the final two chapters of this guide does much to bring the extremes of the debate together. This is an incisive and detailed consideration of a score that adds a powerful aural dimension to a visually vibrant film, but it is also written so that whatever the reader's level of musical knowledge or understanding, there is much to be learned and understood about what part the music plays in capturing the world of Batman.

Dr. Kate Daubney
Series Editor

Acknowledgments

There are a great many people to whom I owe my thanks for their assistance during the course of this project. Chief among these is the editor of this series, Kate Daubney, who first approached me about writing a volume on an Elfman score, and who has been unfailingly generous in her comments and encouragement ever since. Similarly, my thanks are extended to George Caird, Peter Johnson, and Mark Racz at Birmingham Conservatoire for supporting me in terms of both time and resources.

I have received considerable assistance in tracking down the many articles written about Danny Elfman since 1980. Those who have helped me with this are Christian Cooper (*Grammy Magazine*), Matt Gallagher (*Electronic Musician*), Lukas Kendall (*Film Score Monthly*), Ned Torney (*Keyboard*), and the owners of several Web sites: Alicia Armgard (*Boingo 2000*), Thor Haga (*Celluloid Tunes*), Ryan Keaveney (*Danny Elfman's Music for a Darkened People*), and Samantha Paginelli (*Beyond Insanity*).

My family, friends, and colleagues have endured me talking at them about *Batman* for the last two years, and I am profoundly appreciative of their patience and encouragement. These noble souls include Pat and Jim Halfyard, David Saint, Liz Garnett, Shirley Thompson, Simon Hall, Sean Clayton, and Christopher Oakley. Duncan Fielden deserves special mention for his support, his frequently useful comments and ideas, and for his invaluable help in typesetting the book and salvaging the musical examples.

I am indebted to David Olsen at Warner Bros. for his support of the project, and I greatly appreciate the assistance I have received from Daniel Gould and Joseph Bille at the Warner Bros. Music Library, from Matt Smith at International Music Publications Ltd., and from Laura Engels, Mr. Elfman's representative at Blue Focus Management.

Permission to use the following material is gratefully acknowledged:

Extracts from *Batman:* music by Danny Elfman © 1989 Warner-Tamerlane Publishing Corp., USA. Warner/Chappell North America Ltd., London W6 8BS. Reproduced by permission of International Music Publications Ltd. All Rights Reserved.

Extracts from *Batman Returns*: music by Danny Elfman © 1992 Warner-Tamerlane Publishing Corp., USA. Warner/Chappell North America Ltd., London W6 8BS. Reproduced by permission of International Music Publications Ltd. All Rights Reserved.

Chapter 1

Danny Elfman's
Musical Background

Music was a complete accident. . . . I didn't have a plan, so I don't
know how it happened.   —Elfman in interview

Danny Elfman (b. 1953) has been a significant figure in Hollywood film
scoring since 1988, although it was his 1989 score for *Batman* that first
brought him to public attention, in the same way that that film also
marked Tim Burton's arrival as a major Hollywood director. Elfman,
however, has often been regarded as quite a controversial figure in film
music due to his reputation as a self-taught composer and his parallel
career as a rock musician with the band Oingo Boingo. This has led to a
situation where, on one hand, he is one of the most successful composers in contemporary Hollywood and, on the other, he has been pursued
by rumors, widely repeated as facts, that he is musically illiterate. For
many years, he was commonly believed to be not a true composer but
rather a 'hummer,' someone who relies on other people, in particular his
orchestrator Steve Bartek, to turn his ideas into proper musical scores.

The purpose of this volume is to examine in detail the music of
Batman and, in so doing, to examine its composer, his idiom, influences,
working method, and processes of collaboration with both Burton and
Bartek. This analysis aims to cast light upon the modes of production
prevalent within Hollywood film music and the issues that arise within
a musical community that finds itself occupying a sometimes uncomfortable middle ground between the high art of musical composition and
the commercial necessities of the film industry. These issues lie at the
heart of Danny Elfman's legitimacy as one of the most innovative and
meticulous film score composers working in contemporary Hollywood.

Elfman grew up in the suburbs of Los Angeles, the younger son of
two teachers. His mother, Claire (Blossom) Elfman, is also a published
author: her most successful novel is *The Pederast's Wife,* based on the
life of Oscar Wilde's wife. There is a clear family interest in the film and
television industry: Elfman's older brother is Richard Elfman, director

of *Shrunken Heads* and *Modern Vampires*, while Elfman himself has been pursuing a third career as a screenwriter. He has had several projects in development since the mid-1990s, including the musical *Little Demons* with Disney, although none of these projects has reached the stage of production to date. There is also a family history of artistic collaboration between the two brothers and also with their mother, with plans to turn *The Pederast's Wife* into a stage play and a film, to be directed by Richard with music by Danny.

Elfman's Early Career

Elfman's route into film music was far from orthodox. When he was in high school he wanted to be a filmmaker: music was something of an accident. "I imagined myself a cinematographer working toward being a director, or maybe an editor. I always thought that some way or other I'd end up in film, but somehow I ended up in music."[1] Growing up next door to Hollywood, he developed an early love of cinema, and filmmakers and composers he singles out as particularly influential are Ray Harryhausen and his animations alongside Bernard Herrmann's music in *The Seventh Voyage of Sinbad* (1958) and *Jason and the Argonauts* (1963); Hitchcock's films, again with scores by Herrmann; and also the work of Fellini and Nino Rota, including *Satyricon* (1969) and *Amarcord* (1973).[2] Herrmann is clearly a particularly strong influence: Elfman recalls that the score for *The Day the Earth Stood Still* (1951) began his interest in film music:

> That was the first film where I noticed the music and was aware, as a kid, that the music isn't there by magic, that there was a name attached to it. I started to look for that name. . . . It was an awareness that in music there was a difference, there was a personality, an individual, and it made a difference to the film.[3]

His interest in both film music and film itself accounts for the ease with which he made the apparently abrupt transition from rock musician to film composer, with his exceptionally visual appreciation of the medium alongside a musical one: "I've always been more visually inclined. . . . [B]y late high school I wanted to be the new François Truffaut. I wanted to make avant-garde films."[4]

The avant-garde was, in fact, Elfman's initial route into music. He had no formal musical training and did not go to college after leaving high school in Los Angeles. In fact, around the time that he left school in 1971, he had consciously and comprehensively rejected contemporary popular music: "I was influenced in the '60s [by pop music] but when 1971 rolled around, I threw away every album I owned and rejected all my influences and started listening to nothing but Stravinsky and jazz and Indonesian gamelan and developed a whole new set of influences."[5] Elfman is quite specific about the musical chain of events that led to this rejection of pop: "a trumpet player friend of mine turned me on to Miles Davis's *Bitches Brew* and Stravinsky's *Rite of Spring*, and it was probably six short months after that that I threw away almost my entire record collection."[6]

A largely self-taught violinist, trombonist, guitarist, and keyboard player, on leaving school in 1971 he decided to travel the world, taking a violin with him. He had only recently acquired the instrument but took it simply because it was small and light: "I wanted a small instrument to try to learn while I was traveling. Guitar was just too big."[7] Initially he went to Paris where he joined his brother Richard working with an avant-garde street theater group, *Le Grand Magic Circus*. He went on to spend a year traveling through West Africa where he encountered African popular music, in particular the style called Highlife.

Highlife is a twentieth-century African fusion of several different musical idioms that have been finding their way to Africa since the nineteenth century. The hymns introduced by Christian missionaries during the nineteenth century produced a musical idiom that combines European harmony with African practices. The brass instruments of British military bands from colonial days led to the use of brass as the main melodic instrumental group in a typical Highlife band, with the usual regular 4/4 meter, not typical of traditional African music, reflecting the regular rhythm of military marches. This is then blended with polyrhythmic ideas from African traditional music played on percussion in an improvisational idiom that owes a great deal to jazz, which became influential as dance music in Ghana and Nigeria from the 1920s onward.

Highlife later became the model for the musical lineup of Oingo Boingo and led Elfman into a long-standing love of brass and percussion.[8] He has, over the years, collected and constructed a vast array of percussion instruments including African balaphons, a bass marimba, three gamelans—one Javanese, one Balinese, and one he made himself from ground-down aluminum bars—and many smaller instruments.

The Mystic Knights

After a year of traveling, illness led him to return to California where his convalescence took the form of becoming the musical director of the Mystic Knights of the Oingo Boingo. This was an experimental multimedia cabaret act that Richard Elfman had established, based on his experiences with *Le Grand Magic Circus*.[9] Their performances in the United States included a winning appearance on *The Gong Show* in 1976, and the ensemble became the core of Richard's first film project. This was eventually realized as *Forbidden Zone* (1980), for which Danny wrote music and lyrics, as well as being one of its principal performers. The music of *Forbidden Zone* reflects a conscious decision to avoid anything that was obviously related to contemporary pop and rock: the music Elfman was arranging and composing for the ensemble throughout the 1970s, therefore, veers between 1920s' and 1930s' jazz and big band songs and avant-garde musical experiments, the latter influenced by composers from the American experimental tradition, including Charles Ives, Harry Partch, and Terry Riley.[10] Elfman and Leon Schneiderman—a saxophonist and high school friend who had accompanied Elfman on his travels around Africa before they both joined the Mystic Knights—had a shared interest in percussion. Together, they built Elfman's aluminum gamelan and a variety of other instruments such as a 'Schlitz celeste' made from tuned beer cans, turned upside down and played with tiny mallets, and instruments built out of car parts and trash cans, a "junkyard orchestra" as he describes it.[11] This interest very nearly led Elfman into a quite different career as an experimental musician: "I dreamt of following in the footsteps of Harry Partch. And if I didn't become a composer, that's probably where I would've tried to have gone."[12]

It was while working with the Mystic Knights that Elfman taught himself to write music: as he describes it, he ended up being the musical director because no one else could, transcribing Duke Ellington piano solos, Grappelli violin solos, Django Reinhardt guitar parts, and Cab Calloway arrangements.[13] Elfman regards learning to transcribe as a crucial point in his musical development:

> That is where I learned my confidence in my ear. Cab Calloway's arrangements . . . could be very fast and complicated. I would listen to videocassettes of Betty Boop cartoons and old records, but I learned that if I listened hard, I could freeze it in my head and hold it there and write it down. It ended up being critical training for me, even though I didn't know it at the time.[14]

It is apparent from statements such as this that rather than lacking musical training, Elfman lacks only conventional musical education. Lucy Green has written extensively on the differences in how popular musicians learn in comparison to the more formalized process of teaching and learning associated with classical music. In particular she identifies the importance of recordings in the popular music learning process, where the overriding learning practice is that of listening and copying. This therefore contrasts with the pupil-teacher didactic model of traditional instrumental and compositional training.[15] Elfman appears to have acquired what are essentially conventional musical skills such as using notation and transcribing, but has come to this through a typically popular music learning method of repeated, directed listening to pre–World War II jazz. It is unquestionably an unorthodox route for a composer of orchestral film scores but his eight years working with the Mystic Knights enabled him to develop some highly attuned listening skills, most especially the ability to hear internally, and to retain the sound of a complex, polyphonic musical texture in his mind's ear. It was also during this period with the Mystic Knights that he began to compose, effectively extending this skill to capturing and writing down an imagined sound. His most ambitious composition, written toward the end of his time with the Mystic Knights, is the unreleased *Oingo Boingo Piano Concerto One and a Half* for piano and small ensemble. It was the experience of composing this, Elfman has said, that later gave him the confidence to attempt writing for film.[16]

Oingo Boingo

On the completion of the filming for *Forbidden Zone* in 1978, the Mystic Knights officially disbanded, but the musicians, led by Elfman, reformed under the slightly truncated name Oingo Boingo, relaunching themselves as a rock group and releasing their first record in 1979. All but one of the original lineup of the band had played on the soundtrack of *Forbidden Zone,* and both Leon Schneiderman and Steve Bartek were among the musicians who made the transition from the Mystic Knights to the new band. Elfman clearly regarded the transformation of the Mystic Knights into a rock band as a logical and desirable progression: "I had purged all the last theatrical elements [from the Mystic Knights] and we started playing just as a band to see if we could write and perform music without the crutch of theatrics."[17] Oingo Boingo produced a total of twelve albums before finally disbanding in 1995, the best known of which is

Dead Man's Party (1985).[18] Their most commercially successful song was "Weird Science," the title track of John Hughes's 1985 film. Apart from this song, however, the band was practically unknown either nationally or internationally, but they rapidly developed a major following in California that never abandoned them. This was undoubtedly aided by the support and subsequent promotion they received from the Los Angeles radio station, KROQ, and the *Bay Area Music Magazine*, which published interviews with Elfman on a regular basis from December 1980 onward. Oingo Boingo was certainly one of California's most successful and well-known bands throughout the 1980s, despite never truly expanding their fan base beyond the state boundary.[19]

In some respects, Elfman's decision to form a rock band went counter to everything he had been involved in musically up to this point in his adult life but his attitude toward pop changed significantly in 1978. The musical development which reignited his interested in popular music, and which resulted in him writing his first pop songs, was the emergence of British Ska bands, whose music reminded him of African Highlife. "Hearing the Ska that came out of England around 1978 . . . is what turned me around. . . . [Highlife] was a little more Latin than Ska, but really up-tempo. . . . It was hearing The Specials, Selecter and Madness and then XTC, who really clicked for me."[20]

British Ska, like Highlife, is a hybrid of two quite differently located musics, in this case Jamaican Ska and British punk. Like Highlife, it is often typified by up-tempo rhythms and the use of brass instruments, and it is also often characterized by songs that are driven as much by their lyrics as their music. The lyrics of British Ska songs are often narrative rather than the mostly emotionally descriptive lyrics of mainstream pop, and also often demonstrate an overt social and political awareness, an aspect that comes as much from Jamaican Ska as it does from punk.

However, inspired by Ska to start writing songs, Elfman was aware that what he was producing was too different from their existing repertoire to work in the "strange dark cabaret" of the Mystic Knights.[21] Following the decision to disband the theatrical troupe, Elfman's reconstitution of the musicians as Oingo Boingo gave him an opportunity to change artistic direction and concentrate on writing and performing songs in this new context.

Oingo Boingo's music is reminiscent of the kind of eclectic, ironic, self-consciously alternative aesthetic that underlies the work of figures such as Frank Zappa. At the time of the band's formation, live music in Los Angeles was dominated by punk, very different from the often relentlessly upbeat sound of Oingo Boingo's 'new wave' output. Elfman was the founder, songwriter, lead guitarist, and vocalist of the group, which had a basic core of eight members but was sometimes expanded to up to twenty, the performing forces being bolstered by a Highlife-inspired brass section. The eclecticism of Elfman's musical influences, including his interest in film music, is present even in the early years of the band, as this extract from a magazine article of 1980 demonstrates:

> Elfman's music, as interpreted by the seven other members of Oingo Boingo, is a bizarre pastiche of quirky new wave rhythm shifts, Motown-ish horn arrangements, Broadway-musical drama, odd melodic changes worthy of Frank Zappa, gamelan percussion ideas, and barbershop quartet harmonies. In places, their songs resemble DEVO, Talking Heads, even Lene Lovich—but those influences compete for space in Elfman's twisted cranium with the likes of film score composers Nino Rota and Bernard Hermann, [sic] songwriter Kurt Weill, '30s jazz singer Cab Calloway, The Beatles, and The Beach Boys. Oingo Boingo are master synthesists whose melange has all the ferocious intensity of some of the best new wave, but none of its musical predictability.[22]

Most of Elfman's songs are energetic and upbeat, and the lyrics are often blackly humorous, especially with regard to social attitudes, another facet he has in common with Zappa. For example, "Only a Lad," the title track of the band's first album (1981), was inspired by a contemporary news story, and is a satire on the same theme as Bernstein and Sondheim's "Officer Krupke" from *West Side Story* about a juvenile delinquent whose victims and judges decide he cannot be held responsible for his behavior, no matter how unacceptable it is, on the grounds that he is "only a lad."

The particular humor of many of Elfman's songs is also reflected in the album titles, which, as well as *Dead Man's Party,* include *Skeletons in the Closet* and *Dark at the End of the Tunnel*, titles that are indicative of Elfman's blackly comic fascination with the morbid and macabre. This regularly found its way into his song lyrics and was also a major feature of the songs he wrote for Burton's *The Nightmare Before Christmas* (1993). The interest in the macabre extends to his quite extensive collection of occult objects, starting with the juju fetishes he brought home from Mali as a teenager, and now including, among other things, four human skulls, a Tibetan exorcism kit, and an Ecuadorian shrunken head known as 'Uncle Billy,' which received a credit as 'mascot' both on the CD recording of *Batman Returns* and in *Edward Scissorhands*.[23]

Elfman's career as a member of a cult rock band ran in parallel to his career as a film composer for ten years, and it is perhaps initially surprising that a rock musician with no formal training has built his reputation as a composer of large orchestral scores of the old Hollywood school rather than the pop and synthesizer scores that might have seemed the more likely path for him to have followed. He has often appeared ambivalent about his dual musical careers, as revealed in interviews before Oingo Boingo's demise: whichever activity he was currently engaged in tended to involve him so intensely that it would make him wonder what he saw in the other. He characterized his work with the band as full of "energy and sweat" and film composing as a thing of "discipline and concentration," one a communal, collaborative enterprise, the other involving extended periods of solitary work.[24]

The two sides of his musical personality have, in many respects, remained quite discrete, with the rock band not venturing into using obviously orchestral textures until the penultimate album, *Boingo* (1994), and with very few of his film scores using popular music per se: *Midnight Run* (1988), the road movie that did much to revive Robert de Niro's flagging career, uses a blues band ensemble that very much foreshadows Hans Zimmer's score for the more famous road movie, *Thelma and Louise* (1991); *To Die For* (1995) mixes synthesizers, rock, and orchestral elements; and his music for *Dead Presidents* (1995) incorporates the sound of the 1970s' pop songs used in the film with orchestral and synthesizer scoring. Although he has said that he actively dislikes pop scores,[25] there have been other incidents of crossover between his life as a rock musician and songwriter, and his life as a film composer: before writing film scores, he wrote songs with Oingo Boingo for several films as well as *Weird Science,* including *Something Wild* (1986), *The Texas Chainsaw Massacre II* (1986), *My Best Friend is a Vampire* (1988), *Ghostbusters II* (1989), and *Buffy the Vampire Slayer* (1992). In addition, he sang the role of Jack Skellington, as well as writing the music and songs for Tim Burton's *The Nightmare Before Christmas* (1993); and more recently he wrote the additional music for the film version of the musical *Chicago* (2002), the first opportunity he has had as a film composer to draw on his extensive familiarity with 1920s' jazz. However, the majority of his film scores are orchestral and tend toward the quasi-Romantic idiom that typifies the score of *Batman*, the first film in the Burton-Elfman collaboration to achieve blockbuster status, and the sound that has most readily identified Elfman's scoring idiom ever since.

Elfman and Burton

Tim Burton is one of three directors that Elfman has said he would always be happy to work with because of the freedom they allow him as a composer, the other two being Sam Raimi and Gus Van Sant.[26] To date, he has made four films with Raimi—*Darkman* (1990), *Army of Darkness* (1993), *A Simple Plan* (1998), and *Spider-Man* (2002)—three with Van Sant—*To Die For* (1995), *Good Will Hunting* (1997), and *Psycho* (1998)—and ten with Burton. While Raimi and Van Sant regularly work with other composers, Burton has only made one film without Elfman as the composer, namely *Ed Wood* (1994). Following *The Nightmare Before Christmas* in 1993, there was a falling out between Burton and Elfman, the details of which neither has ever been willing to discuss. At the time, it appeared that they had no intention of working together again but their differences, whatever they may have been, were resolved by 1996.

The ten films of their collaboration so far are: *Pee-Wee's Big Adventure* (1985); *Beetlejuice* (1988); *Batman* (1989); *Edward Scissorhands* (1990); *Batman Returns* (1992); *The Nightmare Before Christmas* (1993); *Mars Attacks!* (1996); *Sleepy Hollow* (1999); *Planet of the Apes* (2001), and *Big Fish* (2003). So exclusive a collaboration is a relative rarity in the film industry. Spielberg has worked only with John Williams for most of his career, and Neil Jordan has worked almost exclusively with Elliot Goldenthal since *Interview with the Vampire* (1994), but while a great many directors will make several films with the same composer, these more exclusive partnerships are the exception rather than the rule.[27] The extreme durability of their relationship indicates not only the importance of the collaboration to both Burton and Elfman but also the extent to which a film bearing the Tim Burton name represents more than the vision and talent of one individual, the named *auteur*:

> One might say that the name [Burton] stands equally for the work of the people who have made considerable contributions to what is associated with his name. People like production designer Bo Welch, composer Danny Elfman and graphic designer Rick Heinrichs have been of huge importance to the final product and the Burton concept that has grown from there.[28]

The film that began the collaboration in 1985, *Pee-Wee's Big Adventure,* is a film based on the character Pee-Wee Herrman, created by the actor Paul Reubens for an American children's television program. At the time, Burton was a largely unknown, would-be film director, and he and Reubens were looking for someone other than a traditional Hollywood composer for what is a highly unusual and often very strange film charting the efforts of Pee-Wee to recover his beloved bicycle after it is stolen. Burton had been to Oingo Boingo concerts, while Reubens was one of a relatively small number of people who had seen Richard Elfman's *Forbidden Zone,* and this led to Danny Elfman being invited to write the score for the film. If Burton was expecting an Oingo Boingo soundtrack—and Elfman certainly considered writing something in that style—one can only infer that the director was not disappointed by the score he was eventually given.

Pee-Wee's Big Adventure was followed in 1988 by *Beetlejuice,* although Elfman, ably represented by his agent Richard Kraft, was already writing for other directors. In 1988 alone he also wrote scores for *Big Top Pee-Wee* (this sequel was not directed by Burton), *Midnight Run,* and *Scrooged.* Burton was first approached about making *Batman* after *Pee-Wee* but Warner Brothers only confirmed that the project would proceed following the box office success of *Beetlejuice.*[29] Burton reassembled much of the team from *Beetlejuice,* including the initially very controversial choice of Michael Keaton to play the title role and, in its way, the equally controversial choice of Elfman to write the score.

In the case of Michael Keaton, most of the controversy about casting a short, slender comic actor as Batman was played out before the film's release, and the success of his performance in the film effectively ended the criticism. However, the success of Elfman's score led to a great deal of publicity for him as a composer, and this in turn generated a level of controversy about him that has never entirely been silenced.

The Controversy

For many years, most particularly in the early part of his career, a popular myth has existed that Elfman is a 'hummer'—someone who hums a tune into a tape recorder and then leaves it to someone else to turn this into a workable piece of film music. After the release of *Batman,* a belief emerged—and has persisted—that Elfman did not write his own music, an idea that can largely be traced back to a series of articles and letters published in *Keyboard* magazine between October 1989 and March 1990.[30]

The October 1989 edition of *Keyboard* included an extensive interview with Elfman on the back of the release of *Batman* that summer. Robert L. Doerschuk's introduction to the interview describes Elfman, then aged thirty-six and with only a handful of film score credits to his name, as "an untutored *wunderkind* who's more at home with Performer than with [Walter] Piston."[31] He emphasizes the fact that Elfman's professional musical background was with the "formerly frivolous band called Oingo Boingo," and that:

> Elfman approached *Batman* with credentials that seemed less than ideal. Burton wanted a full-blown orchestral soundtrack, not the electronic reduxes dished out by many of today's young home-brew Hollywood composers. Though self-taught, with none of the conservatory schooling that enables Jerry Goldsmith or John Williams to score for entire divisions of symphonic musicians, Elfman took the gig, cranked up his Mac II, called orchestrator Steve Bartek . . . and eventually came up with what may qualify as the blockbuster soundtrack of the year.[32]

Although Doerschuk appears to view Elfman in a positive light for his own part, the language he uses clearly invites the reader to view Elfman as a controversial figure in a Hollywood film scoring context, a pop musician using technology as a substitute for conventional musical knowledge. Given the nature of the magazine, this is perhaps unsurprising: Elfman's interview is surrounded by advertisements for synthesizers, MIDI systems, sequencers, and samplers, and by presenting Elfman in this way, the interviewer was probably aiming to present him to the majority of the magazine's readership in the most attractive light.[33]

This, however, is largely Doerschuk's own gloss on the interview. In it, Elfman himself is very open about the contributions of others and about his own technical abilities and musical influences. He cites several film composers he admires, including Herrmann, Korngold, and Steiner. When Doerschuk points out that all of these were conservatory-trained, Elfman replies:

> The bottom line is what you hear in your head. . . . I hear orchestral music in my head. . . . The only difference between me and a conservatory-trained person is that I can't analyze why it does what it does.
>
> RD: You say you hear orchestrationally [*sic*]. But can you actually hear specific parts for each instrument in an orchestral score?

DE: It depends. If it's a very rhythmic piece, it's not necessarily that hard. I can retain a lot of music in my head. . . . But there are certain types of music where I've got melodic things working against each other, where maintaining it all in my head gets harder and harder. . . . I can write a fairly elaborate sketch—12, 14, or 16 staves of music—but I depend on my orchestrator, Steve Bartek, to put it into a legitimate context.[34]

What he might mean by 'legitimate context' is another part of the source of the controversy. Without further explanation, it could be assumed he means that Bartek turns haphazard, idiosyncratic notation into workable music. However, orchestrators are widely used in an industry where time is of the essence and, in other interviews, both Elfman and Bartek are very clear that Bartek does not add musical ideas but creates orchestral parts from Elfman's short scores, and he sees his role as completing the tasks an orchestrator would normally expect to perform, such as placing orchestral parts into the correct keys and clefs.[35]

Elfman is also very candid about the contribution of Shirley Walker, the score's conductor, who transcribed the Mantovani-style arrangement of "Beautiful Dreamer" that Elfman incorporated into the score, a musical idea that Elfman freely attributes to Burton.[36] However, the bulk of the interview is a detailed account of musical decisions that Elfman made concerning the *Batman* theme itself and the overall tone of the film score; detailed discussion of ideas related to orchestration; questions related to uses of technology and the integration of percussion samples with the acoustic orchestral music; and the problems that the schedule for completing seventy minutes of orchestral music posed for a composer who was very obviously still at the start of his film scoring career.

The January 1990 edition of *Keyboard* published two letters responding to this article, one a vote of appreciation, the other a letter from composer Micah D. Rubenstein, who was then a professor of composition at Kenyon College, Ohio. Rubenstein was, as he put it, "bothered" by Doerschuk's article because "by glorifying Elfman, he glorifies musical ignorance," and because Elfman's position seemed to him to give ammunition to students who do not see the use or value of learning music theory and compositional technique:

Lack of theory might allow them to play and write bubble-gum rock and roll, but in the complex world of film and orchestral music, there are no shortcuts. If you can't do it yourself, you have to hire competent, conservatory-trained people such as Bartek and Walker to help you.[37]

Additionally, he contests Elfman's lack of training, asserting that Elfman has taken a film scoring course with Christopher Young; and he objects to Doerschuk's use of the word *wunderkind*: "[Mozart] not only heard music in his head, but had the ability and training to write it all down—even complex polyphony and orchestration."[38]

Elfman responded in an open letter that *Keyboard* published in the March 1990 edition. In it, he asserts that he has not studied with Christopher Young or anyone else; that Bartek has never attended a conservatory; and that Walker, like Elfman, considers herself to be self-taught. He objects to what he perceives as Rubenstein's "frightening musical elitism":

> I would guess that it wouldn't surprise you terribly to find out that a respected author may not have had six years of formal English literature, but learned by doing—that is, sitting down at a typewriter and writing, day by day. Certainly you must be aware that there are many film directors—*Batman*'s Tim Burton, for one example—who never attended any film school. Why, then, is it so hard to accept the possibility that someone who works hard can learn to write film music from hands-on experience?[39]

It cannot be denied that Elfman's letter does, at times, descend into rather unexpectedly colorful language. The following quarter, Rubenstein responded in kind in a short, unrepentant letter that perhaps *Keyboard* should not have printed: but given that they had allowed Elfman's unedited and extensive response to Rubenstein, it was too late to start playing censor. The exchange between the two also resulted in a host of other letters, which overall came down a little more on Elfman's side than Rubenstein's. Unfortunately, the damage was already done. Despite, or possibly because Elfman had been open about the contributions of others, the idea that Elfman was not a 'real' composer gained currency. Ironically, Rubenstein's original letter finished by requesting that "when you go up to the podium to receive your Oscar for *Batman*, I hope you'll be honest enough to share it with Bartek and Walker."

The *Keyboard* exchange, coupled with the fact that Elfman was well known as a rock musician in the Los Angeles area, resulted in a widespread belief that Elfman could not have written his own scores, and this probably contributed significantly to the fact that the score of

Batman was not nominated for an Oscar. In fact, none of Elfman's scores from the first decade of his career received nominations. The score for *Big Fish* is the only one of his collaborations with Burton to have been nominated, this being his third nomination. He received both his first two nominations in 1997 for *Men in Black* and *Good Will Hunting*. This double nomination seems to mark the point when Hollywood managed to reconcile its misgivings about Elfman, apparently accepting the evidence that he is genuinely the composer of the music that appears under his name, evidence summarized by Lukas Kendall:

> The similarity of style from score to score, the fact that he has continued to write large-scale scores without using Shirley Walker to conduct, who people at one point assumed really wrote *Batman*; that the scores. . . . Steve Bartek has done on his own have been completely different from Elfman's music; and the sheer illogic to the assumption that Elfman could have hidden an army of ghost-writers somewhere without anyone naming names or coming forward.[40]

In an interview with Kendall in 1995, Bartek talked in detail about the working process involved in being Elfman's orchestrator. Typically, 50 percent of the short score Bartek receives will be from a sequencer, printed off the computer, and the other 50 percent Elfman will have written in by hand.[41] Bartek is also very informative about Elfman's battle with notation, going back to *Pee-Wee*:

> He had a perfectly working knowledge of music notation, because when I joined [Oingo Boingo], he had written [*Oingo Boingo Piano Concerto One and a Half*], fully handwritten for piano and a small ensemble. He considers notation a problem for him, because [of] the fine points of dynamic markings, where they go exactly. He's not good at bass clef, but he does everything in treble clef with an octave marking so you know exactly where he wants it to sound. . . . His notation is not strictly normal, but for anybody who knows anything about notation, you can look at it and figure out what he's saying.[42]

Elsewhere, Bartek has described reading Elfman's notation as being "like reading e. e. cummings. . . . It's different, but not a problem."[43] The fact that Bartek is used to reading this slightly unorthodox notation may be one reason why Elfman has never had to learn standard notation from the ground up; but while it is relatively unusual to encounter an orchestral composer who is not entirely comfortable with the bass clef, Bartek's account makes clear how this problem is resolved. On the subject of whether Elfman composes his own music, Bartek is un-equivocal:

> Lukas Kendall: Danny said, "There's never been a note in one of my scores that I didn't write."
>
> Steve Bartek: Yeah.
>
> LK: Not even a note?
>
> SB: No. An orchestrator's job is to take someone's stuff and make it what the composer wants it to be. In doing that you sometimes 'add notes,' but you don't change melodies, you don't change the harmonic structure, you don't change the composition. . . . [A]t the end of a project when things have to be done, I farm out some of the orchestration, and at certain points we've had orchestrators who have totally changed his stuff, and we've had to re-do it. . . . [They] see them themselves as frustrated composers . . . and like putting their own two cents in somebody else's music. And it just doesn't work with Danny. When he writes down a specific voicing, he wants that voicing. He doesn't want added notes.[44]

Bartek and Elfman also make a distinction between arranging and orchestration: Elfman does the arranging and Bartek does the orches-trating, making decisions about divisions within orchestral parts, and ensuring the full score is legible for the conductor and copyists.[45]

Bartek's role is unquestionably important to Elfman: Bartek under-stands his notation and Elfman trusts him to realize the written score in a way that remains faithful to his intentions. Bartek also has a compos-ing career of his own and one of the most frustrating things for him is the extent to which he finds that directors expect him to write music that sounds just like Elfman's: "they give me this old nudge-nudge that 'you're writing his music.'"[46]

Elfman's talent and the root of his success as a film composer lie in two main areas. First, his visual appreciation of film and his acute musi-cal imagination and inventiveness have given him an exceptional ability to write very effectively against the visual imagery of film, to perceive and capture its tone. Second, he has developed one of the most suc-cessful sets of collaborative relationships with the directors for whom he writes and the musicians who work with him, both in contemporary Hollywood practice and, arguably, in Hollywood's film scoring his-tory. If this kind of collaboration and the music it produces challenge our expectations of what we, as musicians, audiences, and academics, think a nonclassically trained rock musician should be writing for the cinema and how he should be going about it, then we are overlooking the eclecticism of contemporary musical culture itself, not to mention the primarily aural nature of musical experience. The vocabulary of Elfman's music reflects his experience of music, from the late Romantic orchestral tradition that he has come to largely through Golden Age film scoring, to the more atonal and experimental instrumental music of twentieth-century Europe and America, alongside the influence of non-Western musics, popular music, and developments in electronic music (both from a popular perspective and also that of the avant-garde). His early love of film and film music is an important factor in his own approach to scoring: in interview, he regularly mentions the substantial amount of time he spent at the Baldwin Hills movie theater as a teenager, resulting in his love of the scores of the composers such as Herrmann, Rota, and Korngold.[47]

Elfman's own point, made in 1990, about whether we would expect an author to have studied literature in order to be able to write, is apt: as for many writers whose writing is informed by both their own experiences and by what they have themselves read, so Elfman's musical vocabulary is informed by his lived experience of music rather than by formal study. The lack of formal study has clearly not impoverished his imagination in any way and has very possibly enhanced it: he has never specialized in one type of music and so his palette is much broader, and arguably more inventive than that of many of his contemporaries in the film music community.

If the tone of much that Elfman, Bartek, and their interviewers have said about Elfman's compositional practice comes across as noticeably defensive, this is unsurprising given the criticism that has been leveled at him, but it tends to obscure a more interesting and significant perspective on Elfman's contribution to film scoring. In some respects, his working method echoes practices common in the Golden Age of Hollywood film, where the number of films being made and the speed at which they were turned around in production necessitated the existence of studio music departments, staffed by both composers and teams of orchestrators and copyists. Scores were produced as a departmental collaboration and, until 1937, Academy Awards were given to the music department rather than to an individual composer. Elfman's scoring practice is very much a collaborative effort, akin to this in some ways but equally akin to the way that Tim Burton himself works. Where Burton has, throughout his career, consistently gathered around him the same composer, actors, production, and costume designers, so too Elfman has consistently worked with the same orchestrator, Bartek, and has completed around a third of his films to date with the same music supervisor, Bob Badami, as well as working regularly with Shirley Walker in the earlier part of his career before her own composing career developed. As with Burton's work, Elfman's scores are the culmination of a team effort: his is the aural imagination that conceives the moment-to-moment sound of the score, but its realization is part of a more complex collaboration in which all the participants have a claim as part of the Elfman 'brand.'

Elfman could probably work with another orchestrator but he clearly sees no reason why he should: the relationship has worked remarkably well for close to twenty years. Neither seems to feel threatened or undermined by it until they feel they have to start justifying it to critics who, looking in from the outside, try to recast the relationship into a mold that is informed by the practices of concert music composition rather than film music composition. The practices are obviously not the same, although there is a tendency to try and maintain the illusion that they are, to privilege the name of the composer of a film score in the same way as that of a concert hall composer, as if to legitimize film music composition by rendering invisible the differences in its means of production. However, one only need consider the fact that a concert hall composer might be given six months or a year to complete a twenty-minute symphonic composition, compared to the six to eight weeks a film composer might have to complete a seventy- or even one-hundred-minute score, to see immediately that the means of production are dramatically different.

Perhaps because he was unfamiliar with the sensibilities of film score composers seeking to be taken seriously in the musical community at large, Elfman inadvertently created his own problem. By being so detailed about the mechanics of his collaboration with Bartek and Walker on *Batman*, he brought into the open an aspect of film scoring practice that threatened the conventional understanding of the composer as creative artist. The positioning of classical musical composition still conforms very much to a nineteenth-century romantic and early twentieth-century expressionist idea of what the mission of artists should be and what it is that drives them, namely exploring and communicating their inner reality, laying their souls bare to the audience. In this, musical composition is seen as being, by necessity, a solitary act of purely personal creativity that loses its integrity if it is not absolutely truthful: and truth, in this context, corresponds to the direct expression of the individual. Collaboration, therefore, is distrusted on the grounds that this cannot be the composer's true voice if it has been diluted and confused by the voices of others.

Film music, however, is not concerned with the inner reality of the composer as such but with the external reality of the film, and the composer's intentions are automatically subordinate to and informed by those of the film and its director. There is very little sense in trying to make film music stand up to the criteria by which we would judge a contemporary orchestral work and, by the same token, the difference in compositional practices should not necessarily disturb us. The final benchmark by which any film score is going to be judged by its audience is whether it serves the film well. The end is of far more importance than the means and this renders the idea of film scoring practice open to a variety of approaches. At one end of the spectrum there is the music editor constructing a score from existing classical or popular music; at the other is a more conventionally classical model where a single composer is responsible for all aspects of a score's composition and orchestration, a rarity in film music if only because of the complexity of the task and the limitations of time. Between these poles exist a variety of collaborative practices between those with the musical imagination to conceive the sound of a film and those with the technical expertise to realize those ideas. Elfman's output occupies a point in this spectrum of potential practices, and we have only to look at the film scores themselves to see the success of his music in serving the films for which it is written, and to judge the success and legitimacy of the collaborative relationships within which he works.

After the best part of two decades in the Hollywood film industry as one of its most in-demand composers, "a surefire hire in a risk-averse industry,"[48] Elfman is still regarded with a measure of suspicion. He has never tried to hide the fact that his route into film composition was atypical and practically accidental. It could almost be argued that he became a film composer under false pretenses, as it was primarily his work as a rock musician that initially led him to being offered the contract for *Pee-Wee's Big Adventure*, yet he then adopted a very different idiom as a film scorer. This led to suspicions that he could not have composed scores such as *Batman* because he had not come from a background that would have equipped him with the right compositional skills. However, whatever the doubts in the early years about his compositional abilities, it is highly implausible that Burton would have continued to work with him if his was not the musical imagination generating his scores, and it is very much on the back of his collaboration with Burton that his reputation has been built, the working relationship still clearly central to both their careers. Of the films they have made together, *Batman* remained Elfman's biggest grossing film for thirteen years, eventually overtaken by another comic-book superhero film, Sam Raimi's *Spider-Man* in 2002. *Batman*, however, remains Burton's most commercially successful film so far, making an estimated $251 million since its release in 1989.[49] More importantly, this was the film that brought both Burton and Elfman to public attention, and so it is not simply their most successful collaboration but arguably remains their most important one as well.

Chapter 2

Elfman's Scoring Technique

> Question: Why is your music so dark?
> Elfman: Light hurts my eyes.

Danny Elfman has always maintained that his training as a film composer happened in his teenage years during the time he spent at the Baldwin Hills movie theater in the suburbs of Los Angeles.[1] The theater's regular program included reruns of classics from Hollywood's Golden Age, especially horror, fantasy, and science-fiction films, and Elfman actively listened to scores in the context of the films he was watching throughout his adolescence. The effect of this on his approach to scoring is apparent in the evident influence of Golden Age composers, although his approach to the use of themes often goes against the standard practice of the classical Hollywood film score.

Bernard Herrmann, in particular, is a composer that Elfman has always admired greatly and there are interesting parallels in their scoring practice and relationship with the industry, although also some marked differences. Herrmann was highly respected within the industry: he was also known as a composer "who would not be cowed by criticism"[2] and one who frequently took an unconventional approach to his scoring assignments:

> He revelled in the creative possibilities of music, refusing to restrict himself to a single mode of expression or technique, and thus [Herrmann's scoring of *Vertigo*] moves from Wagnerian chromatic harmony, through Pucciniesque diatonic *bel canto* to Schoenbergian atonal *Klangfarbenmelodie*. Although he was undoubtedly influenced by many other composers . . . this should not be taken to suggest that he was simply a talented *pasticheur* only capable of composing through the styles of others, for his is one of the most individual voices in the cinema.[3]

David Cooper's comments about Herrmann could as easily have been written about Elfman, who demonstrates a similar flexibility of idiom and approach in his scores, and yet who, like Herrmann before him, has one of the most individual voices in contemporary cinema.

Genre and Style

When Elfman first began writing film scores, he immediately established himself as a new and innovative voice. The musical idiom of his score for *Pee-Wee's Big Adventure* was inspired by Nino Rota: the bright colors of the visual images and the brightness of much of the music are both reminiscent of Fellini and Rota's collaborations such as *Amarcord*.[4] Elfman's score was noticeably different from the type of music that was being produced for comedies in the 1980s, where a jazz-influenced or synthesizer pop music score—not unlike Oingo Boingo's contribution to *Weird Science*—had become the standard musical idiom associated with the genre. In this context, the fact that Elfman found a different but effective way to score a comic film is the single most important feature of his first score, and it brought him to the attention of other directors. It also indicates the extent to which Elfman has often looked back to film music's stylistic history for his inspiration, reinventing classical scoring ideas for the contemporary cinema.

An immediate result of his contribution to *Pee-Wee* was that until *Batman*, Elfman seemed to be firmly categorized as a composer of comedy scores, as demonstrated by all five of his 1988 projects, *Scrooged, Midnight Run, Hot to Trot, Big Top Pee-Wee,* and *Beetlejuice*. As he himself put it, "all of sudden, it seemed I was being offered every major comedy going through Hollywood,"[5] a situation with which he was not entirely happy as he found most mainstream comedies, unlike *Pee-Wee*, rather limiting from a musical point of view.[6]

Two decades on, Elfman has scored for almost every genre of film being made in Hollywood—even his general objection to scoring romantic comedy was set aside with *The Family Man* (2000) which, although owing an obvious debt to *It's a Wonderful Life* (1947), nonetheless fits quite comfortably into the romantic comedy genre.[7] Throughout the early part of his career, a significant part of Elfman's output continued to be comedy scoring, including *Back to School* (1986), *Summer School* (1987), the five films of 1988, *Pure Luck* (1991), and *Article 99* (1992), not to mention the theme tune for the long-running animated comedy series, *The Simpsons* (1989).

Batman, however, demonstrated a very different type of scoring, a grand orchestral style capable of being both somber and dramatic that was described as 'gothic' by reviewers.[8] Certainly, as will be discussed in chapter 6, much of the music in *Batman* is not unlike the type of music one might expect to find in a horror film and, unlike comedy, this was a genre with which Elfman actively wished to be involved, reflecting his childhood love of monster movies. The success of the *Batman* score and Elfman's own persistence led to him being offered assignments in the horror genre, with the films *Nightbreed* (1990) and *Army of Darkness* (1993).[9] The other main consequence of the *Batman* score is that Elfman has subsequently been asked to write more comic book film scores than any other Hollywood composer, with eight to date: *Batman*, *Dick Tracy* (1990), *Darkman* (1990),[10] *Batman Returns* (1991), *Men in Black* (1997), *Men in Black II* (2001), *Spider-Man* (2001), and *Hulk* (2003). His ninth comic-book film, *Spider-Man II* is expected in 2004: this single genre represents almost a fifth of his scoring assignments to date, creating a strong association between his scoring style and the fantasy action-adventure genre.

Reflecting strongly the types of films that he was being asked to score in the early years of his career, Elfman has two particularly distinct elements in his scoring style, the 'gothic' and the comic, and if one looks at the vocabulary that is regularly used by reviewers and interviewers to describe Elfman's music, one finds two correspondingly broad categories of adjectives that might be summarized as 'dark' and 'quirky.'[11] On the 'dark' side, there are ideas of his music being gothic, intense, and melancholy, while the 'quirkiness' is described using words such as wacky, exuberant, unpredictable, and humorous. However, these two categories regularly cross in the use of adjectives such as strange, disturbing, peculiar, agitated, unhinged, eerie, weird, and twisted, and these are also words that Elfman himself is likely to use in talking about his own compositions.[12]

There is a very distinctive character to much of Elfman's music that results from the juxtaposition of the dark and quirky elements, and the main title of *Beetlejuice* is a very good example of this. The music is in a minor key and has an angular melody played by the brass, the sense of angularity being increased by the repeated use of an augmented fourth. This acts as a constant 'wrong note' that upsets the expected melodic outline and is symptomatic of Elfman's use of dissonance in most of his scores. The dissonance in the melody is underlined by repeated augmented fourth chords from muted trumpets, and these elements would all suggest a sinister tone to the music. However, the rhythmic character of the piece is fast-paced, bright, and dancelike. It has a scurrying, klezmerlike clarinet line and the trumpet motif comes in on a jauntily syncopated offbeat. The juxtaposition of this exuberance with the sinister character implied by the harmonic and melodic material is one of the most characteristic features of Elfman's music. It would aptly describe much of the music he wrote for Oingo Boingo, as well as for *The Nightmare Before Christmas*, and this particular quality is something that has been exploited by directors in a line of films that combine various genres— including thrillers, dramas, fantasy, and horror films—with blackly comic elements. The combination of the dark and the quirky can be found in *Scrooged* (1988), *To Die For* (1995), *Freeway* (1996), *The Frighteners* (1996), and *A Simple Plan* (1998), as well as almost all of Elfman's scores for Burton, the main exception being *Planet of the Apes* (2001).

There is one other category of score assignments that does not fit into any of the genres already mentioned, a series of films that begins with *Sommersby* (1993), a historical drama set in the American South shortly after the end of the Civil War. Elfman's willingness to score the film can be attributed to the fact that it is a love story where the hero is executed at the end, a suitably dark twist that appealed to his love of the macabre.[13] The score is best described as 'bittersweet' rather than gothic and lacks any hint of the comic quirkiness present in much of his other work. Elfman was an unexpected choice for a film such as *Sommersby*, with no history of scoring either historical drama or romantic films, but the result is widely recognized as one of his best scores, probably precisely because it was so uncharacteristic a genre for him to work in and required him to take a new approach. *Sommersby* demonstrated that Elfman could score in a much more understated way and was just as capable a composer away from the action, fantasy, and comedy genres for which he was—and still is—best known. His scores for film dramas, where the narratives and characters are often more complex, are among his best work, including *Dolores Claiborne* (1995) and *Good Will Hunting* (1997). The Oscar nomination *Good Will Hunting* received is probably one of the reasons why Elfman, having spent 1988 composing nothing but comedies, found himself scoring nothing but dramas in 1999, producing scores for *Anywhere But Here*, *Instinct*, and *A Civil Action*.

Like most contemporary composers, Elfman has been accused of repeating himself musically: one reviewer's comment on his score for

Hulk, for example, was that it sounded "like the result of one too many trips to the same well,"[14] and this reflected a general disappointment in the score from many film music critics. This sense of a composer repeating himself or herself is one that is commented on frequently by film music critics, but this is in many respects a current problem of the industry rather than any individual composer: *Hulk* was Elfman's eighth comic-book movie, and his fifth superhero film, and there is a general tendency for contemporary film composers to be 'typecast.' Elfman happens to be strongly identified with this genre because, having written a couple of very successful scores for Burton's two *Batman* films, other producers and directors have looked to him as someone with a proven track record of writing this kind of score, in preference to an established composer who has no association with the genre but who might well have something new to contribute. As Jeff Bond describes it, "we have reached a stage today where . . . the pressure to recoup costs [is] so staggering that experimentation and new approaches are not only difficult to mount, but are in most cases actively discouraged. The job is to recreate the sound of the last successful action blockbuster."[15] The thinking is often that the best person to do this is the composer of the previous score, as is overwhelmingly apparent in the last-minute choice of Elfman to write a score for *Hulk* to replace the original score by Mychael Danna. This typecasting undoubtedly underlies the reason for Elfman's spate of comedy scores in the late 1980s and spate of dramas in the mid-1990s. Most members of a film's audience are not studying the soundtrack and so are less aware—and less concerned—that a composer may be reusing the same kinds of themes and textures that appear in previous scores in a similar genre. Elfman is acknowledged as an important and innovative composer whose scores for *Beetlejuice*, *Batman*, and *Edward Scissorhands* have had a lasting influence on contemporary scoring, but there is probably a limit on how original any composer can be if repeatedly called on to write scores for fundamentally similar films.

Theme and Tone

Elfman's tendency to structure most of a score around variations of a single theme has also occasionally caused criticism of the album releases of his scores where, removed from their visual context, it becomes much more apparent that the material used in many of the cues is actually very similar. However, within the context of the film for which it was written, the thematic material helps to impress the tone of the film on the viewer, creating a sense of atmosphere and identity that goes beyond the localized events of individual scenes.

In many of the projects Elfman has undertaken since 1985, the starting point—particularly when he is working with a director he has worked with before, such as Burton or Raimi—has been to visit the set during production, where he starts to get a feel for the visual identity or 'tone' of the film: this is something he has been doing on Burton's films since *Beetlejuice*.[16]

From comments given in interviews in 1990 and 2002, it is apparent that Elfman's development of musical material and the process of mapping this against the film became established early on and has changed very little over the course of his career.[17] Initially, he experiments to find themes that capture the tone of the film, its overall emotional, psychological, and dramatic feel as he perceives it to be conveyed by the director's visual language. He normally hopes to have two to four weeks to do this, although production overruns and other unforeseen circumstances sometimes reduce the amount of time available.[18] This is a very methodical, controlled process, a studied preparation for the work to come, immersing himself in the sound world of the as-yet-unwritten score and familiarizing himself with its timbres and themes:

> A painter friend of mine . . . once brought me to his studio, and he was setting up all of these jars of pigments and colors. I asked him what he was doing and he said "I've been doing this for about a month. . . . I don't start a painting until I've settled on exactly what tones and pigment and colors [I'm using and they] are compared and laid out in a certain fashion. When it is completely done, I'll start my first picture." I thought to myself, "that is exactly what I'm doing when I start a film." I'm laying out all my melodic pieces, knowing in my head how it is all going to work together.[19]

As a major part of this preparatory process, Elfman will choose three or four key scenes from different points in the film—usually the beginning, middle, and end—and test how well the material works in context against the image.[20] The way that themes are used within Elfman's scores generally relies far more on variation than on repetition, and so an important aspect of the development of his musical material for a film at this stage is finding themes that will work well in a variety of transformations, themes that:

can be turned a number of different ways. I'll take the theme and figure out whether I can play half of it and still recognize it. Then, does it work in a major and a minor key? Can I turn it from funny to spooky? Can I cut it down to just three notes and still make it recognizable? These are some of the acid tests I put a theme through while I'm composing.[21]

He also brings the director in around this time, to ensure that he or she is also happy with the core musical material. In the case of *Batman*, the person who needed convincing at this stage was not Burton but the producer Jon Peters:

> I had written all this dark music, and Jon Peters was saying "look, this is fine, but you know, we're talking about a *hero* here!" I played him all these pieces . . . but, at this point, it was essential that I came up with this one heroic theme. I just took the same basic theme and turned it into this march, and did it a certain way—changed the key around a little bit—and all of a sudden [Peters] leapt up out of his chair and it was completely obvious that I had found the *Batman* hero theme.[22]

Once the developmental phase is complete, he will have reached a situation where several key sections from the film have been clearly defined in relation to the thematic material, which will have been thoroughly explored to establish the different ways it can be used and transformed and what these individual transformations signify in the score as a whole. This use of thematic development is a feature of Elfman's scoring, which connects his technique back to the Golden Age composers he so admires. Scores such as Herrmann's *Vertigo* (1958) and *Psycho* (1960) both demonstrate the way that large amounts of differentiated musical material can be generated from single themes, from inverting a thematic idea to imply a reversed narrative position or emotion, to using a theme to generate ostinati and other accompaniment figures, all of which are features that can be found in the score of *Batman*.

Having established the material of the score, Elfman then turns back to the beginning of the film and begins to work through it chronologically, using the material he has developed in a manner he describes as "organized chaos" in comparison to the more methodical process of developing the material:

> Once I have all [the thematic] elements together, there is no method anymore. I just dive into the first cue. I go as close to chronologically

as I possibly can. I don't plan or think about where the music is going
to go. It really is extremely unmethodical. I tend to let the music carry
itself, and I become very often surprised by it. I never question it.[23]

An example of the kind of musical surprise that results from this intui-
tive approach to the composition of the score occurs in *Sleepy Hollow*.
Here, the principal theme is that of the Horseman but the subplot, which
generates a second theme, is Ichabod Crane's memory of his childhood,
his mother, and his gradual retrieval of the facts of her death. However,
although they initially start as two distinct themes in Elfman's scheme,
they are used apparently interchangeably in the score:

> On a literal level, it makes no sense that the same theme that is
> playing over Ichabod's flashbacks as a child is also playing over the
> Horseman . . . but sometimes the Ichabod theme would just pop up
> and we'd have to play it. I never resist those things. . . . If it works, I
> don't question why."[24]

Nevertheless, it is quite possible to read this use of the 'wrong' theme in
a logical and meaningful manner. Both the main plot and the subplot are
bound up with dark forces, witchcraft, and death. The Horseman theme
is used for the Horseman, the supernatural threat he poses, and the fear
he inspires. The second theme is associated specifically with Ichabod's
memory of his mother's death but more generally with memory and
mystery: things unknown and needing explanation, things that are not
understood by those who see them, and things that are remembered
and recalled, especially when those memories are not entirely revealing.
As a result, it tends to be found in the flashback sequences, but it also
occurs in relation to the Horseman because the reasons for the murders
he is committing are mysterious, while the truth of his death is concealed, just as the circumstances surrounding how and why Ichabod's
mother died are a mystery. The music is working to link narrative
ideas at a level rather more sophisticated than simply having a theme
to represent the Horseman and one to represent Ichabod, although they
do work as character themes in relation to their orchestration. The
Horseman's music, regardless of which theme is being used, is characterized by male-voice choir, brass, pipe organ, and low strings. When
the memory theme is used for him personally, it tends to be delivered
with a brass *fortissimo*, compared to the delicate, ethereal orchestration
and children's voices used for Ichabod's memories of his mother. There

are some strong narrative ideas underlying why it makes musical sense to use the second theme for the Horseman's character and, although Elfman's compositional use of the theme demonstrates that he is aware of this intuitively, he clearly does not feel the need to articulate these ideas at a conscious level. As a composer, Elfman knows what does and does not work: even when he is surprised by the results and does not entirely understand them, he is happy to trust his instincts and leave analysis to the analysts.

It is the desire to capture the tone of a film that results in Elfman's scores often being dominated by a single theme, as heard particularly distinctly in both *Batman* and *Edward Scissorhands*. This theme sums up the holistic idea of the film, creating a strong musical identity for it, and while his treatment of the theme connects him to the Golden Age composers, the number of themes he uses clearly differentiates him from them. In particular, his approach rejects Max Steiner's idea that every character should have its own theme, a widely agreed maxim that regularly produced half a dozen different themes in typical classical Hollywood scores. A similar principle underlies the scoring of contemporary composers such as John Williams and Elliot Goldenthal, whose scores may have six or more identifiable themes. Very few of Elfman's scores, especially since *Batman*, have more than three themes, and several of them have only two, which between them generate all the material of the score through statement of the themes, their fragmentation into motives, and other forms of variation. Like *Sleepy Hollow*, many of his scores fall into a pattern of having a principal, unifying theme, found in the main title and dominating the score thereafter; and a secondary theme, which may be used only occasionally for a contrasting narrative idea that works against the main tone of the film and its corresponding theme.

This pattern of scoring can be heard in the music of Elfman's other Oscar-nominated score, *Men in Black* (1997). Here, the two themes are the rhythmic, funky bass theme that, like the film itself, owes not a little to *Mission: Impossible* (which Elfman had scored, using Schifrin's TV theme, the previous year), and a more reflective, lyrical theme. All the activities of the main characters in pursuing their goals tend to be accompanied by the first theme and its many variations, regardless of who the character is. The lyrical theme, meanwhile, is used for rare moments of reflection about the sacrifices that have to be made in order to be one of the Men in Black, the loss of loved ones, and the isolation from normal life. In tone, these scenes are quite different from the rest of action-oriented material and act as a subplot that makes the agents a little more human and emotional, and this difference in tone gives rise to the secondary, contrasting theme.

Other scores demonstrate that Elfman's concept of theme is not always primarily melodic: in *Batman Returns*, for example, each of the three principal characters—Batman, Catwoman, and the Penguin—has their own theme, but the themes are actually remarkably similar and are arguably all variations of each other. Catwoman and Penguin have themes whose basic motives are identical in their proportions, with the first four notes simply inverted; all three themes are in a minor key; and all three begin by describing a minor third interval (figure 2.1).

Figure 2.1a: The Penguin's Theme
Danny Elfman, Batman Returns *Recording, "The Lair"*

Figure 2.1b: Catwoman's Theme
Danny Elfman, Batman Returns *Recording, "Selina Transforms"*

The difference between these themes is found less in their melodic content than in their orchestral treatment and demonstrates that rhythm, gesture, and timbre are often more important than melody in differentiating thematic ideas in Elfman's scores. For Catwoman, Elfman used what he describes as a "1960s' slinky, bending style of strings,"[25] and the use of high string *glissandi* and dissonant clusters are the defining characteristic of her theme. Batman, as in the previous film, has brass as his primary instruments. The Penguin, meanwhile, is given the most theatrical music, complete with a chorus of voices against pipe organ and full orchestra, lending his music "a grand, overblown quality that was sometimes just plain sinister."[26] However, the similarity of the three themes also serves to underline one of the main narrative ideas of *Batman Returns,* as they correspond to the three dual-personality principal characters. A theme of the film is that these characters are in many respects very similar, three people who have suffered some great trauma and as a result have developed an animal alter ego who either rises above the trauma to fight for good or becomes a vengeful, embittered, and possibly insane villain, this being a classic comic-book convention in the formation of superheroes and their archenemies. The underlying similarity of the three characters in *Batman Returns* is reflected in the way Elfman scores them, furthering both the narrative and the sense of musical unity in the score.

Orchestration and Idiom

The musical sound world most clearly associated with Elfman is that of the dark, orchestral scores that he has written principally for Tim Burton. The key features of this 'gothic' idiom are the very prominent use of minor keys, low-pitched melodies and textures, and frequent use of dissonance at both melodic and harmonic levels. Jeff Bond identifies Elfman as "one of the few members of the new generation of [Hollywood] composers who regularly applies atonality, dissonance, and sonic experimentation to their scores,"[27] and this is a feature of all his scores, not just those written for Burton.

Minor keys are more or less ubiquitous in his music for Burton's films: with the exception of *Pee-Wee's Big Adventure*, which constantly switches between major and minor keys, none of the main titles or principal themes of any of his scores for Tim Burton is in a major key. However, although much of his reputation has been built on his collaboration with Burton, this accounts for only a fifth of his film scoring between 1985 and 2003. While this particular sound world is also largely characteristic of his scores in fantasy and horror genres, many of his scores in other genres and for directors other than Burton bear little obvious idiomatic resemblance. This includes the comedy scores he wrote between 1985 and 1989, including *Midnight Run*, and many of the scores he has written since *Batman* for nonfantasy dramas. In particular, the scores for *Sommersby*, *Dolores Claiborne*, and *Good Will Hunting* do not strictly adhere to the pattern of minor keys and low-pitched melodies, and they demonstrate Elfman's versatility and musical breadth in capturing the tone of films that are very different from Burton's fantasies. The types of themes he composes will obviously have an impact but, as outlined above, texture and timbre tend to be as thematically important as melody, which gives a high importance to orchestration in establishing the tone of the music and the film.

The characteristic distribution of the orchestra and the roles played within it in Elfman's Burton scores typically place the melody in the middle or toward the bottom of the texture, played by brass, low strings, and low woodwind. Higher-pitched instruments, such as violins, flutes, and oboes, which might traditionally expect to be the principal melodic instruments, tend to become the main means of pacing the texture, where a sense of speed and energy is created by rapid countermotifs in strings and high woodwind, one of the best-known examples of this being a composition for someone other than Burton, namely the theme tune for *The Simpsons*. The creation of a sense of energy and movement through the layering of textures and the foregrounding of low-pitched, brass- and percussion-heavy melodies against busy accompaniments that are often much higher pitched can be found in all the Burton scores from the main titles of *Beetlejuice* and *Batman* to a cue such as "Ape Suite No. 2" from *Planet of the Apes*, where almost all the material is low-pitched.

This is a technical aspect of Elfman's writing that breaks with some long-standing traditions relating to instrumental pitches and the voices of the actors. One of the reasons that it is more usual to find melodies in the higher ranges in classical Hollywood scores is the fact that they are then further removed from the pitch of the actors' and actresses' speaking voices, so avoiding the possibility that the music might either obscure the dialogue or be obscured by it. Concentrating on lower-pitched melodic lines effectively gives an alternative solution to the same problem, in that the melodic line is usually removed from the pitch area occupied by the voices but in the opposite direction to that dictated by convention. However, this is not always the case: in *Batman*'s "Descent into Mystery," the musical material, in particular the choir, is pitched at exactly the same level as Kim Basinger's voice, and Elfman thins the texture considerably when she speaks to prevent one interfering with the other.

The general exception to the rule of where the melody lies is seen most clearly in the main title cues of both *Edward Scissorhands* and *Sleepy Hollow*: when important themes are pitched in the upper register, they tend to be taken by what are often thought of as two of Elfman's scoring trademarks, by the voice itself, and by celeste. This lends a very specific quality to his higher-pitched melodies, giving them a slightly unearthly and eerie ambience. The celeste, like the harpsichord, has an inhuman quality about it, perhaps stemming from the extent to which the human player cannot significantly influence the quality of the sound being produced. This has resulted in these instruments acquiring a particular cinematic musical coding. The harpsichord is very much associated with evil, amorality, and sinister calculation as seen in scores from John Addison's *Sleuth* (1972) to Wojciech Kilar's *The Ninth Gate* (2001). The celeste, on the other hand, with its pure, music-box, bell-like quality, has come to be associated with memory, mystery, and things not truly of this world. This is present to some extent in its use (via Bartók's *Music for Strings, Percussion and Celeste*) in Kubrick's *The Shining* (1980), and it is firmly established in Elfman's vocabulary, where it often represents characters whose sense of innocence stems from the fact that they are so far removed from our own reality that they are potentially a little frightening: Edward Scissorhands is the most extreme example in this category.

The use of voices, particularly women's and children's voices, has a similar effect. Children's voices are often found in films concerned with dangerous, supernatural, or alien 'others,' from Walter Schumann's *The Night of the Hunter* (1955), to Lalo Schifrin's *The Amityville Horror* (1979), and Elliot Goldenthal's *Interview with the Vampire* (1994). All these films, like *Sleepy Hollow*, have children as important characters and, on one level, the children's voices in the soundtrack are specifically linked to and representative of the children in the narrative. However, in all these films, the apparent innocence of the child's voice is positioned against the threat implicit in the film's title and genre and, by association, the child's voice itself comes to represent that threat, conveying a sense of mystery and immanent evil. Elfman has used voices regularly throughout his scoring career and, given these associations, the presence of voices is a symbolic element of the darkness of many of his scores, even when the pitch and timbre of the voices themselves are high and bright. In *Edward Scissorhands*, as in many of his other fantasy-genre scores such as *Scrooged*, the wordless boys' choir lends the film a sense of warped Disney scoring, managing to evoke something of the use of choirs in films such as *Pinocchio* (1940), on which the film as a whole is clearly modeled, and *Sleeping Beauty* (1959), with its Tchaikovsky waltz rhythms: but this is Disney seen through a glass darkly, the major keys of the voices in those films replaced with the minor-key waltzing of Elfman's main title.

The register and timbre of voices is all-important: adult choirs and male-voice choirs, as found in many scores including *Batman* and *Sleepy Hollow*, have a more obviously dark sound compared to the higher registers and lighter, brighter timbres of children's voices. Significantly, in the aforementioned Disney scores, children's voices are not heard in the nondiegetic singing: "When You Wish upon a Star" and "Once upon a Dream" are both scored for adult SATB choirs. However, when Elfman uses adult voices, the lower registers and darker timbres are used to convey a sense of threat. A clear example of this is again found in "Descent into Mystery" where, as the Batmobile hurtles through darkened woods, the wordless choir acts to heighten our anticipation and Vicki's dread of what lies ahead. In general, the lower the register, the more threatening the musical result: in *Sleepy Hollow*, a male-voice choir in its lowest possible register is used in the main title to create one of Elfman's most sinister cues to date.

Leading on from this, one of the generally innovative features of Elfman's music is the extent to which he chooses a distinctive and sometimes very unusual palette of instrumental colors for each film score, an attention to timbre that is perhaps a legacy of his Harry Partch–inspired instrument-building years, but which is also another example of Herrmann's influence. David Cooper notes that:

> Herrmann's orchestration was often eccentric: the "Sleigh Ride" from *The Magnificent Ambersons* is scored for three glockenspiels, two celestes, piano, two harps, small and large triangles, and jingles; *The Day the Earth Stood Still* uses two theremins, electronic violin, bass and guitar, four harps, four pianos, percussion, and brass; *Psycho* is scored for string orchestra.[28]

Some of Elfman's timbral choices are quite intentional acknowledgments of Herrmann's orchestrations: *Dolores Claiborne* uses a large string orchestra in a direct reference to *Psycho*'s use of strings, while *Mars Attacks!* adds a theremin to its frequently atonal scoring in an homage to *The Day the Earth Stood Still*.[29] Although many of Elfman's other scores use a fairly conventional orchestra, there will usually be a particular weight given to certain key instruments, or the addition of particular instruments to the standard orchestral forces, such as *Edward Scissorhands*' voices and celeste, and *Sleepy Hollow*'s solo child's voice. In *Planet of the Apes*, the orchestra is highly unusual, consisting of a large brass section, no woodwind, no violins, six violas, four double basses, and twelve cellos. This ensemble is then augmented with an enormous amount of percussion, a decision that initially suggests a reference to Jerry Goldsmith's percussion-based textures in the original film of 1968. However, Elfman's orchestration of the film is very different, in part because seventy-two tracks of the percussion in the final mix are contributed by Elfman himself, using his own samples, and also because Goldsmith complemented the percussion writing with highly textural, atonal writing for the rest of the orchestra. Elfman's orchestra, however, is pared down to brass and strings, which are then given a decidedly subordinate role to the percussion.

The principal themes of the Burton scores are always on a grand scale both orchestrally and thematically, to the extent that they verge on parody, the basic idea writ so large that there can be no mistaking that this is Comedy, or Gothic Adventure, or Fairy Tale, or Sci-Fi, or Horror (to describe *Pee-Wee, Batman, Edward Scissorhands, Mars Attacks!*, and *Sleepy Hollow* respectively). Elfman speaks the language of film music's codes of signification with such fluency that in Burton's films he is able to concentrate existing signifiers into a musical form that captures the tone of the film so well that it effectively redefines the music of an entire genre, as has happened in particular with his early comedy scoring, the music of *Batman* in comic-book and action-adventure genres, and *Edward Scissorhands*' post-Disney redefinition of the idea of fairy tales and fantasy.

In contrast to the extraordinarily dense and dark scores written for Burton's films, Elfman's other scores often occupy very different musical territory, although the underlying approach to scoring is similar. In particular, the selection of a specific palette of colors plays an important part, and a brief survey of his other work makes it apparent that Elfman is capable of abandoning the dark, brass- and percussion-dominated scoring that is so closely associated with him. Although he often uses his own percussion samples in the recordings of his scores, he generally avoids using synthesizers, although there are some prominent exceptions: *Wisdom* (1986) has an eighty-minute score entirely played by Elfman on synthesizers, while *To Die For* uses self-consciously sampled and synthesized sounds for the artificially glamorous world of its ambitious and unscrupulous heroine. *Sommersby* uses an acoustic guitar as one of the principal melodic instruments; *Black Beauty* (1994) draws on folk dances and instruments, especially fiddle and pipes; *Instinct* augments the orchestra with an ensemble of nine flutes and a detuned piano; *A Civil Action* is scored mainly for strings and woodwind but also makes considerable use of bowed and struck glass, which Elfman felt worked well as a musical metaphor for the importance of water in the film's narrative.[30]

If the instrumental timbres being explored in his scores for directors other than Burton are sometimes quite different, so too is the nature of the music being written, although a connecting thread is the predominance of minor-key themes, reflecting Elfman's love of writing melancholic music.[31] In *Dolores Claiborne*, the orchestration concentrates on strings

as primary carriers of both melody and texture and, as noted above, Elfman has acknowledged that the use of an orchestra dominated by strings
is a tribute to Herrmann's *Psycho* score, the connection being that like
Psycho, Dolores Claiborne is a film about murder, an old woman living
in a large and isolated house, and the problematic relationship between
a mother and her child, although the eventual outcomes of *Dolores
Claiborne* are considerably more optimistic than those of *Psycho*. There
is very little use of woodwind and brass in Elfman's score and, when
it is used, it tends to be used to fill out the texture rather than to carry
the melodic line. The piano is the only instrument outside the string
family to have any kind of major role in the orchestration and, unlike
the Burton scores, there is no significant role for percussion here. The
idiom of the score varies between the largely tonal, elegiac, broodingly
melodic writing of the main title and the anxious, dense, atonal textures
of cues such as "Getting Even" and "Ferry Ride" that sometimes sound
not unlike the string writing of mid-twentieth-century such as Ligeti
and Lutoslawski. Even in the more tonal music, Elfman makes great
use of unresolved suspensions to create discords in the melodic line that
undermine the music's tonal center. Elfman regularly uses tonality itself
as a code, and threats to tonal stability often correspond to dangers and
disturbances within the narrative, as they do in this score.

Good Will Hunting is another atmospheric score that in many respects is the antithesis of the Burton works. This is a score utterly devoid
of the grand theatrical gestures and dramatic themes at which Elfman
has proved himself so adept. Instead, Elfman has written a chamber
score, albeit with a fairly eclectic combination of instruments: piano,
flute, oboe, pipe, guitar, some percussion, occasional strings, very occasional brass and—Elfman's signature—a boys' choir.

The texture of the score is highly distinctive, a fluid interweav-
ing of separate motifs played by single instruments, which might be
compared to the loosely interlocking patterns of John Adams's *Shaker
Loops* (1983). This might account for why some commentators have
described this score as minimalist. In a certain sense, it is: clearly, it
is composition with minimal means compared to the grand orchestral
style of some of Elfman's other films. However, the score bears the clear
imprint of Elfman's scoring technique, placing the emphasis on capturing the global tone of the film and on the careful creation of a timbral
palette for the score that will serve this tone. On a practical level, the
timbral palette of the score, particularly the use of the acoustic guitar,
was a conscious decision to enable the score to merge seamlessly with

the songs by Eliot Smith that are used at several points. This is quite an unusual approach to the relationship of pop songs alongside an orchestral score and some of the segues Elfman writes using the guitar are so carefully integrated with Smith's songs that it is difficult to tell exactly where the cue ends and the song begins.

This score is not readily recognizable as the 'Danny Elfman sound' except possibly in the brief sections using children's voices. Again, in keeping with how voices are used in other scores, their presence also signifies that while Will is hardly a child or innocent in any conventional sense, it is the process of uncovering the truth of his childhood that is the key to the narrative's resolution. In terms of capturing the tone of the film, the score is innovative and highly effective. The main title sequence refracts the visual image, producing kaleidoscopic images of its various shots; the music, in turn, is 'refracted,' each of the instrumental lines separated out from each other and moving in musical space like elements of a Calder mobile, creating some prolonged moments of dissonance as the musical elements cross each other's paths. [32] This serves as a metaphor for the life of the central character and the life of his mind, with all the different and often conflicting ideas that characterize him: the purity of his intellectual abilities against the chaos and unhappiness of his emotional life; his genius set against his violence. The nature of Will Hunting is reflected in the audible process of musical elements coming into focus, losing cohesion, refracting again, and ultimately finding some level of resolution in a very carefully crafted and subtle score.

The tone of the film and the character of Will Hunting himself are potentially problematic. Will has a tendency toward violence, antagonism, and aggression, and he is also a mathematical genius: as he negotiates his journey toward self-knowledge, it would be very easy for him to come across as arrogant and unsympathetic. Elfman's music goes a long way toward mediating the less agreeable aspects of his character in the way that the score avoids heavy, orchestral textures and large musical gestures. The extreme quietness of the score, the delicacy of the textures and gestures, and the use of the children's voices instead give Will a childlike quality and innocence that both make him more sympathetic and lend credibility to his psychological breakthrough at the end of the film where the true cause of his violent behavior, the trauma of his childhood, is finally revealed. The music has led us to this moment, continually pointing to the fact that, at some level, Will is still locked in a child's incomprehension of the world around him.

Elfman is a very adaptable composer and while his scores for Burton share a similar darkness of tone, this is not the only color on Elfman's palette even if it is the one for which he is best known. His decisions regarding themes and orchestrations are made consciously in the service of the film and with the intention of capturing its all-important tone, which is perhaps why the Burton scores do all appear to have an identifiable 'Elfman sound' that is sometimes less apparent in his other films. The tone of Burton's films is very consistent: they are, for the most part, darkly comic fantasies that are concerned with the bizarre and the macabre, and they are not set in the world as we know it. Given the underlying similarity of Burton's films, it is unsurprising that there is a certain similarity of tone in many of Elfman's scores for this particular director.

Chapter 3

The Historical and
Critical Context of *Batman*

The Changing Face of Batman, 1939–1989

The Comic-Book Superhero

The superhero is, on the face of it, a twentieth-century invention of the comic-book genre, the world's first superhero being Superman, who arrived in June 1938 in *Action Comics* No. 1. Created by two Jewish high school friends as "a calculated response to the Nazi concept of the *Übermensch*" on the eve of World War II, "Superman was a uniquely American *Übermensch* with a social conscience."[1] His appearance—a dark-haired figure dressed in the red and blue of the American flag—sets him in automatic opposition to the Aryan supermen of Nazi ideology, while the naming of Superman appropriates and subverts the Nazi interpretation of Nietzsche's creation. Nietzsche's Superman himself points back to an earlier superhero prototype, that of Wagner's Siegfried, and it is Siegfried who in turn connects the idea of the superhero back to the panoply of ancient mythological heroes, with the quests and missions of Jason and Ulysses, battles against the forces of evil, such as those of Beowulf and Theseus, and epic tales of impossible strength, such as the labors of Hercules.

Although Superman emerged as the first comic-book superhero of the twentieth century, Batman was a close second. Created by the graphic artist Bob Kane and the writer Bill Finger, he appeared just under a year after Superman in May 1939 in *Detective Comics* No. 27. Just as Superman's mission and appearance had their origins in quite specific sources, so Kane cited the inspiration for Batman in two early Hollywood films. From *The Mask of Zorro* (1920), starring Douglas Fairbanks, came the basic Bruce Wayne formulation of a "wealthy landowner who maintained both an alter ego as a masked and caped crimefighter, and a secret cave-hideout beneath his mansion."[2] The appearance of Batman and the darker side of his character came from *The Bat Whispers* (1930), in which the central character is a detective with a problematic dual identity. This schizophrenic split creates "The Bat," a murderer whose favored manner of dress directly inspired the Batman costume.

As well as the inspirations cited by Kane, elements of several other fictional heroes can be identified in the construction of Batman. The pulp fiction character, the Shadow, is a psychic thief turned crimefighter who again reflects some of the divisions and conflicts in Batman's character and his ambivalent relationship with the law. Sherlock Holmes and the comic strip character, Doc Savage, both fall into the same category as Batman as "master sleuth and scientist"; and another comic strip character, Dick Tracy, shares with Batman a square jaw, a youthful sidekick and a "cast of bizarre villains."[3]

The characters, events, and vocabulary of Batman's world (or 'continuity,' as it is referred to in comic-book circles) were established very quickly. The famous Bat-prefix (e.g., Batcave, Batmobile) dates from 1939, the first year of Batman's comic-book life. Robin first appears in 1940, the Batmobile in 1941, and Alfred in 1943, while Catwoman, Penguin, and Two-Face all appear between 1940 and 1942. Gotham itself does not appear at the outset: Batman's city was originally Manhattan, and some of the early comic-book stories are located in Metropolis, Gotham becoming his permanent home in 1941.

The Joker is Batman's first regular adversary, appearing in *Batman* No. 1 in the spring of 1940, but his origins were not fully explained until February 1951. This marks one of the first major deviations in Burton's *Batman*: in the comic-book continuity, the Joker was never the killer of Bruce Wayne's parents, and his transformation into the Joker resulted from his own miscalculations without any involvement from Batman. This is one of the reasons why comic-book fans, while generally approving of Burton's film as being true to the spirit of *Batman*, decided that it did not form part of the *Batman* continuity. It is generally accepted among fans that any *Batman* story line can add to what we know about the characters but should not contradict events or knowledge established in earlier adventures. Such contradictions, unless they can be adequately explained, fall outside the official continuity of the *Batman* macronarrative, and this is the position of Burton's film, with its deviations from established elements of Batman's biography.

The Caped Crusader versus the Dark Knight

Where Bill Boichel identifies some of the inspirations of Batman in contemporary films, fiction, and comic strips, Will Brooker sees in him strong resonances of James Bond, vampire mythologies, and Robin Hood. His connection to Robin Hood lies in "both characters' ambiguous relation to society" as members of the dominant class who operate outside the structures of the law, while Batman's connection to vampires is that of "a gothic figure whose identity is subject to transformation."[4] This similarity is made even closer by the fact that Batman's transformation, like Dracula's, is specifically a transformation into a bat, operating within a nocturnal environment.

Batman's similarity to Bond lies less in the nature of the characters themselves and more in their adaptability to changing times, with a variety of different Batmen and Bonds capable of reinventing and modifying themselves for new generations in new media, resulting in "different Bonds [and Batmen], popular in different ways and for different reasons at different points in time."[5] This observation is especially relevant in the context of the 1960s' television series. Bond has been through a variety of incarnations and cultural positionings in literature and film, the most dramatic shifts being from the ruthless but suave agent of the 1950s and '60s to the camp parodying of Bond in the 1970s and the self-assured irony of the 1990s. The ABC television series made between 1966 and 1968 represents a similar shift in Batman's position—one that is generally held to be an aberration by comic-book fans, which can be traced in part to the way that comic-book style is parodied in the unique televisual vocabulary of this series, particularly in the fight scenes.

It was also greatly resented by many fans that the series positioned Batman in the realms of camp and comedy, one result of this being to reinforce the idea that Batman and Robin are gay. This idea had first emerged in 1954, when Frederic Wertham, a psychiatrist involved in the treatment of homosexuals, published *Seduction of the Innocent*. His work focused mainly on the malign influence of horror comics on impressionable children and on the connection between comic books and delinquency, racism, and anxiety about body image and sexuality in both male and female adolescents. In the context of sexuality, he included a quite lengthy discussion on the homoeroticism of Batman's relationship with Robin. Wertham's main concern was that this relationship led to young men identifying with Robin and being drawn into fantasies about Robin's relationship with Batman. This could, in turn, lead to feelings of guilt, confusion, and anxiety about their sexual orientation and might even provide a stimulus to an adolescent's latent homosexuality. An immediate result of Wertham's research was his involvement with the U.S. Senate Subcommittee hearings in 1954, which investigated the link between comic books and delinquency. This led directly to the formation of the Comic Magazine Association of America that year, a self-regulatory body that created the Comics Code, a similar code of practice to the film industry's Hays Code.[6]

However, although Wertham was very cautious in his comments and surprisingly unhomophobic for his generation, the suggestion that Batman and Robin are a gay couple outraged Batman's heterosexual fan base and inspired ridicule from many writers on popular culture. Conversely, the inference that Wertham was attacking homosexuality led to outraged denunciations of his work by queer theorists in the 1990s.[7]

Meanwhile, Brooker observes that just as "Wertham is detested by fans for his role in bringing the 'gay Batman' reading into public circulation, so Adam West's TV show is disliked for its part in playing up to that interpretation."[8] With its absurd, overblown villains and often ludicrous dialogue, littered with rhyming couplets, excessive alliterations, and Robin's infamous expletives prefixed by the word 'holy,' the 1960s' Batman is a long way from the 1930s' original who witnessed the death of his parents, and whose crusade against crime is a "personal vendetta"[9] born out of a traumatic obsession.

In the 1980s, the comic book reclaimed Batman from the screen and distanced him from the camp and comedy of his 1960s' incarnation. Frank Miller, author of two of the most famous *Batman* graphic novels of the time, *The Dark Knight Returns* (1986) and *Batman: Year One* (1988), was particularly influential in repositioning Batman as a darker, more threatening figure. This was a version with which his creator, Bob Kane, pronounced himself happier than he had been with television series, which he described as "marvelous spoof." Miller's Dark Knight, he felt, "returned to my original conception of Batman as a lone, mysterious vigilante."[10] Miller's *The Dark Knight Returns* and Alan Moore's similarly positioned *The Killing Joke* (1988) are the strongest comic-book influences on Burton's 1989 *Batman,* both in terms of the film's visual and narrative tone, and also in terms of some plot elements.[11] However, the character of the Joker is also a throwback to the camp of the 1960s, thereby juxtaposing different facets of Batman's historical identity within the cinematic space of the narrative.

Burton's Batman

The two words that seem to occur most frequently in describing both
Batman the film and its score are 'dark' and 'gothic,' and to some extent
these words are used interchangeably. In terms of the visual appearance of the film, there is a very literal justification for the use of these
adjectives. Most of the narrative is set at night, the natural habitat of the
bat, and the few daylight scenes are dull, overcast days without a hint
of sunshine.[12] Similarly, several of the locations—Wayne Manor and
Gotham Cathedral in particular—have a gothic architectural appearance, while the name of Gotham City itself appears to make an allusion
to the gothic.[13]

The idea of darkness is carried over into the colors associated with
various characters. The minor characters, such as Knox, Eckhardt, and
the family lost in Gotham at the film's opening, are generally dressed
in undistinguished, uncolorful shades of brown, while Vicki Vale and
Bruce Wayne are usually dressed in black and white. Only the Joker
consistently uses color, most notably purple or blue for his clothing,
and green for his hair, and it is perhaps significant that the only time
Vicki wears color, she finds herself in trouble. She wears a blue dress for
her supposed date with Bruce at the museum, but instead finds herself
with the Joker. Wearing color, she puts herself into his territory, makes
herself vulnerable to him, and has to be rescued by black-clad Batman.
The dark-gothic-Gotham formulation also gives a clear indication of to
whom Gotham really belongs. The Joker may want to own the city, but
his use of color positions him as an outsider and usurper of Gotham's
true son and heir, Batman-Bruce Wayne, with his penchant for black
and his mask's resemblance to the cathedral gargoyles.

On the subject of the visual identity of the film, one has to wonder
when exactly the narrative is set, as the film gives out a series of comprehensively and intentionally mixed messages. Grissom and Napier
are essentially coded as 1930s' gangsters, with their double-breasted
suits and Fedoras. Likewise, the newspaper reporters and the police all
seem to be part of that same era, with hats and trench coats that mark
them out as more contemporary to Philip Marlowe and Dick Tracy than
NYPD Blue. Equally, the newsroom inhabited by Knox and Vicki is
furnished with old-fashioned wooden desks and typewriters: there is
no chrome, no plastic, and no computers, making it more like the newsroom of the original Clark Kent than of his modern film incarnation.
The lost family that opens the film is clearly also of the same era; and

the flashback sequence of the murder of Bruce Wayne's parents is again consistently coded for the 1930s, from the clothing and hairstyles of all the characters in the scene to the design of the popcorn bags.

By contrast, the TV news presenters are very much of the 1980s, as it would clearly be more difficult to make a television studio appear anything other than modern. The female presenters have classic 1980s' power suits and shoulder pads; the suit worn by their male colleague lacks the obvious 'period' features of the gangsters or the newspapermen. Vicki, whose femaleness makes her seem to have more in common with the female TV presenters than with the all-male world of the journalists, moves between these visual codings. She does not appear out of place in the newspaper office—her hem lines are generally long—but also tends to wear clothes not out of place in the 1980s, such as the previously mentioned blue dress and the outfit she wears to dinner at Wayne Manor. Much of her clothing, however, is neither explicitly of one era nor the other.

Bruce Wayne also moves between these temporal positions. His childhood memories of himself are of the 1930s, but his adult incarnation is generally seen formally dressed and so it becomes more difficult to establish exactly 'when' he is. Sometimes he could be coded for the 1930s, such as when he appears in his black overcoat outside the museum during the Joker's attack on the other mob bosses. However, unlike the other men in this scene, he wears no hat and so appears more modern. Similarly, the gray suit he wears in scenes at Wayne Manor is slightly ambivalent, but the cut is too close to the body to evoke the squarer shape of a 1930s' jacket. Apart from the television newsreaders, only Bruce and Vicki appear to inhabit the modern day, so emphasizing them as the characters with whom we should be identifying the most, and further distinguishing Batman from the Joker.

The mixing of these time frames also helps to create a mythic level to the narrative, removing it from any specific time or place. As Uricchio and Pearson observe:

> Unlike some fictional characters, the Batman has no primary urtext set in a specific period, but has rather existed in a plethora of equally valid texts constantly appearing over more than five decades. This has freed him from temporal specificity.[14]

This lack of temporal specificity is also exploited in the film's locations. Wayne Manor itself is very much of the 1930s—complete with butler—but the frame from which Bruce hangs upside down in his bedroom is clearly a modern contraption. The Batcave beneath the Manor is full of technology, including the chrome and computers that the news office lacks, locating the cave as a 1980s' structure that lies beneath the 1930s' environment. The only occasion we see Bruce Wayne out of a suit, overcoat, or formal evening wear but not in the Batsuit is in the cave, where he wears a black sweater and jeans. This is visually slightly shocking, being so unambivalently of the 1980s, but appropriate therefore in reinforcing the difference between the Manor and the Batcave, as well as adding a new dimension to the relationship between Bruce and Batman. This is the scene in which Vicki finally discovers the truth about Bruce's other identity and so this is the only scene in which it is unclear whether we are seeing Batman out of his Batsuit or Bruce Wayne out of his formal clothing.[15] Instead, we meet a third persona, the respective 'masks' of both Batman and Bruce removed, revealing a man who is neither one nor the other but the true synthesis of them both.

Batman himself, however, largely exists outside the temporal locations: there is no era in which contemporary fashion has included body-molded rubber suits. His use of technology identifies him with the 1980s, while the suit serves to make him gothic, statuesque, and almost architectural, the musculature of his body revealed and exaggerated like a sculpture cast in black, topped by a gargoyle's head. The Batmobile also echoes the gothic-meets-art-deco architecture of the city museum with its long lines and abruptly curved edges, both of these again identifying Batman as part of his city.

This juxtaposition of the 1930s and 1980s in the film has a certain logic. In Burton's film, the temporal layering, seen most graphically in the relationship between the Manor and the Batcave, serves as a metaphor for how the original idea of Batman exists alongside the more modern idea of the Dark Knight. The 1930s' images relate the narrative back to Batman's original 1939 comic-book incarnation, while the 1980s' clothing brings it into the decade contemporary to its audience. At the same time, the 1960s' rendering of Batman is referenced in the Joker's campiness, his grimly comic quipping and occasional use of rhyming dialogue, alongside his use of slightly tacky, joke-shop props such as the toy pistol that fires a little flag saying 'bang,' a direct allusion to the television series' use of graphic intertitles for its sound effects.

Superheroes and the Fantasy-Action Film Genre

The superhero started with—and to a greater extent still belongs to—the comic-book genre. Of the vast number of comic-book superheroes, only a very limited number have been translated into screen formats. Superman, Spider-Man, Batman, Wonder Woman, and the Incredible Hulk have all had successful TV series, although only Superman survived beyond the 1980s, with *The New Adventures of Superman* and more recently *Smallville: Superman—The Early Years.* Animation, with its more obvious connection to comic-book graphics, has continued to pursue superhero-style narratives for children, from *G-Force* and the *Teenage Mutant Ninja Turtles* in the 1980s to *Pokemon* in the 1990s, and these narratives in turn generated some live-action series, still aimed at children, such as *Power Rangers.* These creations have mainly emerged from Japan and Taiwan, and from the same places have come the main superhero-type animation genres aimed at adults, Animé and Manga. However, during the course of the 1990s, mainstream television drama largely lost interested in comic-book heroes, replacing them with other forms of fantasy adventure as found in science fiction (*The X-Files, Star Trek: Deep Space Nine,* and *Star Trek: Voyager*), myth (*Xena: Warrior Princess* and *Hercules: The Legendary Journeys),* and magic (*Buffy the Vampire Slayer, Angel,* and *Charmed*).[16]

In the cinema, until very recently, only a limited number of characters have appeared on the big screen. Superman once more demonstrates the seemingly endless appeal of a fundamentally uncomplicated man leading an extraordinarily interesting life: Superman's first cinema appearance dates from 1948, not in a film but in a fifteen-episode serial. His first genuinely filmic appearance starts and finishes in the quartet of Christopher Reeve films spanning 1978 to 1987. However, perhaps a little surprisingly, Batman outdoes him on all fronts. Batman had two cinema serials, the first dating from 1943, with a sequel, *Batman and Robin,* in 1948. His first film (1966) resulted as a spin-off from the 1960s' television series, followed a generation later by the *Batman* quartet, which spans the years 1989 to 1997, albeit with two different directors and three different Batmen.

However, other than these two, there is a distinct lack of comic-book superheroes in the cinema before 1989. Spider-Man, the next most popular of the early comic-book characters, had to wait until 2002 for a cinema appearance and Wonder Woman is still waiting, although Supergirl put in an appearance in 1984.

The evidence seems to indicate that superhero narratives are not a naturally cinematic genre. Given the wealth of comic-book characters and story lines available, already presented in a strongly visual and dialogue-driven format, it is surprising that so few of them have been translated into film narratives. However, if one looks at certain film narratives, it is apparent that although the comic-book characters themselves have only appeared relatively rarely on-screen throughout most of cinema's history, the way that comic-book superheroes are constructed has a strong similarity to the construction of the action heroes in science-fiction and fantasy action-adventure films of the late 1970s and 1980s, including some of the most popular film 'franchises' of the time, George Lucas's *Star Wars* trilogy, Richard Donner's *Superman* and its sequels, and Steven Spielberg's *Indiana Jones* trilogy.

There are certain characteristics of comic-book superheroes, categorized by Richard Reynolds, that provide a working definition of the superhero genre.[17] The main points of these categories can easily be seen in the way each of the central characters of *Star Wars*, *Superman*, *Batman*, and the *Indiana Jones* films is constructed, demonstrating how much they have in common with their comic-book counterparts.

First, there must be either lost parents and/or a complicated relationship with them. Superman, Batman, and Luke have all lost theirs, although Luke's relationship with his father becomes complicated when he is revealed to be Darth Vader. Indiana's father is absent for the first two films, is lost at the start of the third, and then turns up later on as an uncompromisingly problematic father, who humiliates his son by revealing that Indy's real name is Henry, while Indiana was their pet dog.

Second, the superhero must stand for justice, frequently putting him over and above the law. Superman and Batman find themselves occupying a potentially precarious position between the law and crime, but choose to ally themselves with the former; Luke opposes an Empire that has lost its moral and, therefore, legitimate authority; Indiana stands as a representative of truth, justice, and the American way in his regular confrontations with the Nazis. This is a dimension that gives him a clear underlying link to the origins of Superman, although he also seems to set himself above the law with his legally dubious archaeological raiding trips in search of buried treasure.

Then there must be superpowers or their equivalent. Superman is clearly more endowed with superpowers than anyone else is, and Luke has his Jedi Force. Batman is famous in superhero circles for having no special powers: he is human, unlike Superman—and, in fact,

Luke—and instead he relies on gadgetry as a superpowers equivalent. Likewise, Indiana Jones, although dealing with the supernatural, also relies on gadgetry, especially his trusty whip, making him curiously reminiscent of Wonder Woman in this context.

There must also be a secret identity, a double life. Hence, we have the Clark Kent–Superman and Bruce Wayne–Batman formulations as the classic examples, but Indiana Jones has one life as a bow-tied and bespectacled college professor and another as an intrepid archaeologist, while Luke varies the theme again by having a second identity that is not immediately revealed to him, namely that he is the son of his own archenemy and brother to Princess Leia rather than the simple farm boy he always believed himself to be.

Additionally, and relating directly to the earlier point about justice, the superhero is positioned in contrast to politics and the law, where the expedience and ineffectiveness of legitimate authority forces the super-hero to act illegally to ensure justice. So, Indiana is forced to attempt to steal the Grail, the Ark, and other artifacts in order to prevent them from falling into the hands of the forces of evil; Luke is forced to join the rebellion against the Empire; and Superman and Batman are both forced into vigilante action that initially arouses suspicion in the media that they may be as bad as the criminals.

It is apparent from this that cinema has responded to the superhero as constructed by comic books, both by adopting their most successful pair of characters and by inventing their own heroes for action adventures that have strong elements of fantasy in them, including hypothetical futuristic civilizations, the 'magic' of both technology and the supernatural, and narratives that pursue relatively uncomplicated battles between the forces of good and the forces of evil.

The fact that there is no true comic-book film genre is born out to a certain extent by the remarkably inconsistent and varied terminology used to categorize films that fall into the action-adventure category and also contain comic book–style superheroes. To take the categorizations used by the *Radio Times Guide to Film*, *Star Wars* (1977) and *Return of the Jedi* (1983) are both described as science-fiction fantasy adventure, although *The Empire Strikes Back* (1980) is a science-fiction epic; *Superman* (1978) is a fantasy adventure, while *Batman* is an action fantasy; and *Raiders of the Lost Ark* (1981) combines both of these to be an action-adventure fantasy.[18] The connecting element is quite clearly fantasy: this appears to be the true cinematic equivalent to the comic book genre.

Burton's *Batman*, however, marks a moment of change in the cinematic approach to the fantasy superhero. The cinematic superheroes of late 1970s' and 1980s' cinema emerged from a cultural and economic climate sunk deep in recession: both Europe and the United States suffered from record levels of unemployment in the late 1970s, resulting in the toppling of the socialist government of Jim Callaghan in the United Kingdom and the liberal government of Jimmy Carter in the United States by the right-wing capitalists Margaret Thatcher and Ronald Reagan in 1979 and 1980 respectively. In this climate of economic uncertainty, it is not surprising that Hollywood should turn to a series of emotionally uncomplicated, all-action superheroes, men who could save the world. The recently reinstituted title of the first *Star Wars* film, *A New Hope*, makes this even more explicit and explains more clearly why the *Star Wars* epic started at a point halfway through the story, rather than with the three films that had to wait another twenty years to be produced. The trilogy starting with *The Phantom Menace* (1999) is much darker, the heroes, most notably Anakin Skywalker, more flawed and complex than the boyishly innocent Luke or the charmingly reckless Han Solo. The cinematic heroes produced by the recession—Luke, Superman, and Indiana Jones—are all essentially optimistic characters, full of life and energy, with enormous capacities for love, impulsive acts, and an altruism that generally appears quite effortless.

Burton's *Batman* emerged at a quite different point in the Western world's economic history. *Batman*, coming to the screen in 1989, did so long after the World Recession had been left behind, to be replaced by the 'Greed is Good' culture that flourished in the mid-1980s' economic boom. However, a cynical and distrustful attitude rapidly emerged toward this culture, as seen in Caryl Churchill's satire on Thatcherism's values in the play *Serious Money* (1986), and in films such as *Wall Street* (1987) and *Working Girl* (1988), both of which serve as indictments of their central avaricious characters, as played by Michael Douglas and Sigourney Weaver.

In this climate of disillusionment with the less pleasant side of human nature when it finds itself in possession of (economic) power, a new kind of hero was called for, one who could still save the world but whose relationship with power made him less susceptible to its potentially corrupting influence. It was the very optimism of the 1980s' boom years, the sense that the economic boom was such a good thing that simply getting more of the same could not be bad, that led to what came to be perceived as an unhealthy self-interest that ignored any idea of the greater good. For the

empowered to be able to work for the good of all rather than only themselves, the relationship with power itself must not be allowed to become
comfortable or seductive: the hero must, to some extent, be unwilling.

Batman is the ideal hero for such times. His is a fundamentally
unworldly character: although he is wealthy, his wealth is inherited and
he therefore cannot be accused of being personally implicated in its
acquisition; and our first sight of Bruce Wayne is at his charity ball,
making his philanthropy explicit. In fact, he is rendered tragic by his
wealth as this, in combination with his lack of family, has isolated from
the normal run of society, leaving him to live practically alone in a
mansion so vast that there are rooms he has never been in before, as
is revealed in the dining room scene with Vicki. Unlike the heroes of
the 1980s, he is also a fundamentally pessimistic character. Having lost
his parents so young and in such terrible circumstances, he resists the
attempts of others to get close to him and is wracked by indecision about
whether to get involved with Vicki. He cannot freely embrace his power
as superhero but hides it behind a mask, keeping the heroic identity so
secret that it threatens his chance of happiness with her.

Duality and Dysfunction

The darkness of Batman as compared to Superman, although emphasized by Burton, has always been part of his mythology, a deliberate attempt from the outset to create a character that contrasted significantly
with Superman.[19] Superman is an alien, Batman is human; Superman
seeks to help humanity because he can, Batman exists as the result of a
traumatic personality split, creating an alter ego who is driven to right
wrongs and so assuage the guilt of the child who could neither save his
parents nor die with them. From the start of their comic-book existences,
Batman has always been a much darker, less comfortable character than
the supremely reassuring Superman. The superhero outfits they wear
are almost identical in cut, but Superman's is made in bold, primary
colors, and he wears no mask. Batman's colors have been muted grays
and blacks even in his most brightly colored 1960s' incarnation and the
mask, as likely to indicate a bank robber as a superhero, has always been
firmly in place. This contrast extends even to their environments. Den-
nis O'Neil describes Gotham as "Manhattan below Fourteenth Street
at 3 a.m., November 28 in a cold year," while Metropolis is "Manhattan
between Fourteenth and One Hundred and Tenth Streets on the bright-
est, sunniest July day of the year."[20]

The darkness in Batman's character also creates a potential in him to be a villain rather than a hero and, in the two *Batman* films directed by Burton, much is made of the thin division that separates Batman from the villains, perhaps even more explicitly in *Batman Returns* than in the first film. Again, this emphasizes the extent to which Batman is in constant conflict with his power: Luke Skywalker is only seriously tempted to give in to the unrestrained power of the dark side of the Force on one very specific occasion in his final confrontation with Darth Vader and the Emperor; Batman, on the other hand, constantly seems to be holding himself in check, forcing himself to hand villains over to the police rather than simply dropping them off the side of buildings, the idea of restraint further suggested by the visual metaphor of the bondage imagery inspired by the famous rubber suit in which Burton encases him.

Another aspect of Batman's essential pessimism is that, as Boichel points out, from the very beginning of his continuity "many of his villains [have] mirrored aspects of Batman's character and development."[21] This is seen in the way that both he and his opponents have all been created through emotional or physical trauma. Superman was born the way he is: it is earth's gravity that makes his dense molecular structure result in apparent superpowers. Not so in the *Batman* continuity or in Burton's narrative. Joker and Catwoman's trauma is physical (a fall into a vat of chemicals and being pushed out of a skyscraper window respectively), while Batman and the Penguin's trauma is emotional, both involving the loss of parents. Batman's are murdered in front of him and the Penguin is rejected and abandoned by his. They effectively try to murder him by casting his pram adrift in a storm drain, unable to cope with his terrifying nature, which is seen as synonymous with his deformity: we have seen his clawlike baby's hand reach out and kill the pet cat in the preceding scene.

Reynolds describes Batman's villains as possessing "qualities which . . . derive from a radical inability to function in the everyday world—in short, sketches of various types of madness" and he goes on to point out that "this madness is a part of Batman's special identity . . . [his] obsessive character links him with his enemies."[22] Certainly, Superman's opponents are quite different from Batman's. In Richard Donner's film, Lex Luther is evil but slightly comic and wears a wig, although he is obviously a physically normal human being; and while the Krypton trio of the second film are corrupted by power, they are not insane so much as utterly seduced by their sense of superiority and invincibility. All of Batman's opponents, with the exception of Catwoman, are physically bizarre, and this spills over into manifestly bizarre behavior: they are not simply morally corrupted by power but rendered holistically abnormal by it. Bruce-Batman himself is not immune to this process. Batman, molded by the rubber suit and mask into a parody of his human self that conjures up images of bondage, bank robbers, vampires, and gargoyles, has a physically extreme appearance and displays obsessive behavior in his drive to impose his version of order on Gotham. This, therefore, connects him to the physically and behaviorally bizarre criminals who seek to impose their own order on the city, and the one thing that saves him from being truly like them is Bruce. The Joker cannot take off his mask any more than can the Penguin. Catwoman can, and Selina is the reason that Catwoman is able to function as the potential love interest in the second film, being most like Bruce-Batman himself. Bruce, meanwhile, is the counterbalance to the madness that threatens to consume Batman. In contrast to the latter's focus and obsession, Bruce is endearingly absentminded and vulnerable, giving Bruce-Batman the capacity for the normal human identity that Selina-Catwoman so nearly yet so tragically fails to achieve. The Joker and the Penguin can never attain this, Jack Napier and Oliver Cobblepot having been completely subsumed within their alternate identities.

The superheroes of the late 1970s and 1980s discussed here are all much more creatures of the light than Batman. Although all of them are tempted at some point—Luke by the dark side of the Force, Superman by wanting to win Lois by revealing his true identity, Indiana by the lure of the treasures he seeks—there is never any serious likelihood that they will succumb to these temptations as they are simply too unlike their enemies, too sunny of disposition, too essentially full of the joys of living to be corruptible.[23] Bruce Wayne is not like these people: he is a traumatized human being whose isolation from normal life has left him with very little understanding of the real world he seeks to protect. He stands as close to the villains he opposes as it is perhaps possible to stand without becoming one of them.

The Influence of Burton's *Batman*

In terms of *Batman*'s lasting influence on Hollywood cinema, there have been some obvious comic book–inspired films that mirror both the campiness and comic book color of the Joker, foremost among these being *Dick Tracy* (1990), *The Mask* (1994), and *The Phantom* (1996).

However, it is the conflict in the character of Burton's Batman that has most profoundly altered the idea of the hero in fantasy and action film narratives since 1989. Batman's darkness, the idea of a superhero who is complex, problematic, pessimistic, and introverted, has been frequently revisited. The emulators of Luke Skywalker, Indiana Jones, and Superman were characters such as the relentlessly upbeat and noble *Flash Gordon* (1980), and the energetic teenage heroes of *The Last Starfighter* (1984) and *Back to the Future* (1985). *Darkman* (1990) and *The Shadow* (1994) reflect the problematization of the superhero, both films taking comic book–type characters and narratives that place the superhero in the same ambivalent vigilante position as Batman between the forces of law and those of crime.

He is also arguably an antecedent of the complex, initially unwilling superhero Thomas Anderson-Neo in *The Matrix* (1998), as well as the darkly aggressive hero of *Blade* (1998), films that owe as much to *Batman* as they do to *Terminator* (1984). In many respects, *Terminator II: Judgment Day* (1991), where the 'supervillain' android returns, newly transformed into superhero, explores the same dualistic formulation of Batman's conflicted personality. Given that seven years separate the original *Terminator* from its sequel—an inordinately long time in Hollywood for a hugely successful film to wait to take advantage of the sequels market—it would be pleasing to think that *Batman*'s popularity may have played a part in bringing the reconstructed Terminator back to the screen. Similarly, the upsurge of superhero narratives after *The Matrix* may account for the decision to bring the Terminator back in a third film in 2003, reaffirming the android's place in the canon of superheroic film characters.

Batman's influence continues in a new generation of comic-book films taking advantage of developments in computer-generated effects to realize superheroic feats in the cinema. These films include *X-Men* (2000), *Spider-Man* (2002), *Daredevil* (2003), *Hulk* (2003), and *The League of Extraordinary Gentlemen* (2003), all of which still owe more to Batman than to the earlier generation of optimistic heroes. Ang Lee's Hulk is seen as a victim of his internal duality, to the extent that he cannot function as a superhero but instead tends to destroy everything around him. The League is a recent comic-book invention made up of nineteenth-century literary characters, several of whom border on the monstrous in their dual natures, including Dr. Jekyll, Mina Harker as vampire, Dorian Grey, and the Invisible Man. Magneto, played by Ian McKellen in *X-Men*, is a representative of what happens to the Batman-type superhero when he gives in to the 'dark side,' while all the mutants on the good side are deeply conflicted in ways not unlike Batman himself, seeking to protect a world they cannot properly inhabit, both because society rejects them and because, due to their differences, it is a world they cannot truly understand, being unable to participate in its most rudimentary behaviors. Rogue is unable to experience any form of physical contact without injuring or killing the person she touches; Cyclops cannot look anyone in the eye without burning them to a cinder. Similarly, Daredevil's blindness creates a barrier between him and the rest of the world, and he is presented in the film as a driven and self-destructive character who, like Batman, needs love to bring about his salvation.

Spider-Man, on the face of it, has far greater potential as a straightforward, optimistic superhero in the Luke Skywalker mold, and indeed, Tobey McGuire has an only slightly less conventionally attractive boyish charm to match the young Mark Hamill's, coupled with the vaguely nerdish awkwardness of Michael Keaton's Bruce Wayne. However, once again, the narrative problematizes his relationship with his powers, reducing the likelihood that he will be lulled into a complacent attitude toward them and be tempted to use them for personal gain rather than for the good of others. The device used to achieve this is the death of his grandfather: Peter Parker is cheated of his winnings by a wrestling match organizer and so does not use his superpowers to protect the man when a thief bursts in. Instead, Peter lets the thief escape, a decision that leads directly to his grandfather's death at the thief's hands. Peter then turns vigilante, hunts down and kills the thief—not entirely intentionally—realizing only at the last moment that it is the same man he allowed to escape earlier. This sequence of events tarnishes the pleasure he had previously taken in his powers and awakens in him the knowledge that with them comes responsibility, and that he is capable of doing great harm if he acts in his own self-interest.

Batman is unquestionably a major cultural icon. The Batman logo is so instantly recognizable after more than sixty years in the public domain that the DVD issued by Warner Bros. does not even have the title *Batman* on its front cover, merely the Bat-symbol in its golden oval frame; and Neil Hefti's theme tune for the 1960s' television series is similarly an instantly recognizable signifier of Batman. For those who are not part of the comic-book community, two starkly different images of Batman prevail in the public imagination: the camp humor of the 1960s' series, and the darker, grimmer world created by Tim Burton, which has influenced both the subsequent films by Joel Schumacher and the Warner Bros. animated series. Both these ideas of Batman coexist within the range of texts that make up Batman's cultural identity but, in the last fifteen years, the 1960s' Caped Crusader has become part of the backward-looking culture of kitsch and nostalgia, while the 1980s' Dark Knight of Burton's cinematic version has gone on to have a far-reaching impact on Hollywood's superheroic narratives.

Chapter 4

The Sound of the Score

Batman's Music

Tim Burton's *Batman* is a total of 121 minutes in duration.[1] Of this, just over eighty-four minutes contains music, which is almost exactly 70 percent of the film (table 4.1 gives a breakdown of all the music used). Ten minutes of this is accounted for by songs written by Prince; another four minutes consists of excerpts from Mozart's *Eine Kleine Nachtmusik*, easy-listening arrangements of Max Steiner's theme from *A Summer Place* (1959), Stephen Foster's "Beautiful Dreamer" (1862), and an extremely brief quotation, sung by the Joker, of "A hot time in the old town tonight" (Hayden and Metz, 1896). All of this material is diegetic, which leaves a fraction over seventy minutes of music composed by Danny Elfman, almost all of which is nondiegetic. Overall, this represents a high proportion of screen time supported by music, and the *Batman* soundtrack reflects the trend toward increasingly high proportions of music in film. In the 1960s and 1970s, the standard length of a score was between forty and sixty minutes, although there are many examples of much longer ones. Since the early 1990s, the idea of a forty-minute score in a mainstream film is practically unthinkable and so little music would probably automatically qualify the film for art-house status. By way of contrast, Jerry Goldsmith's score for *The Illustrated Man* (1969) is forty-two minutes long and Jerry Fielding's score for *Demon Seed* (1977) is under forty minutes, as is Johnny Mandel's highly influential score for *Point Blank* (1967).[2] Throughout the 1990s, the tendency toward almost continuous music steadily increased, to the extent that *Batman*'s seventy-minute score is quite short in comparison to that of *Sleepy Hollow*, which occupies eighty-five minutes of a film only 101 minutes long.

Table 4.1 Musical Material in Batman

Score Cue	Title[3]	Duration[4]
1m1	Titles (short)	2'30"
	Prince: "The Future"	36"
1m2–3	Family—1st Bat	1'54"
1m4	Roof Fight	1'13"
2m1	Jack vs. Ekhart	1'29"
2m2	Up Building	9"
2m3	Card Snap	1'34"
	Prince: "Electric Chair" and "Vicki Waiting"	2'47"
3m2	Batzone	1'12"
4m1	Axis Setup	34"
4m2	Shootout	5'21"
4m3	Untitled (Segue)	12"
4m3a	Kitchen Dinner	1'07"
5m1	Surgery	1'26"
5m1a	Stair Kiss	14"
5m2	Face Off	2'08"
5m3	Beddy Bye	1'28"
	Hayden & Metz: "A hot one in the old town tonight"	4"
6m2	Roasted Dude	54"
6m3	Vicki Spys	1'41"
6m4	Clown Attack	1'50"
7m1–7m2a	Bruce Contemplates/Photos	2'45"
7m3	Men at Work	26"
7m4	"Wild"—TV News Theme	7"
7m5	Joker's Commercial	1'17"
7m6	Paper Spin	4"
8m1	Alicia's Mask	19"
	Mozart: *Eine Kleine Nachtmusik*	46"
8m3	Vicki Gets a Gift	1'05"
	Prince: "Partyman"	1'34"
	Steiner: "Theme from *A Summer Place*"	1'21"
8m6	Alicia's Unmasking	59"
8m7	Rescue	43"
8m8	Batmobile Chase	2'25"
9m1	Street Fight	54"
9m3	Descent into Mystery	1'25"
9m4	Bat Cave	2'22"
9m5	Paper Throw	11"
	Foster: "Beautiful Dreamer"	1'39"
10m3	Joker's Poem	50"
10m9	Sad Pictures	33"

11m1	Challenge/Dream	2'53"
11m2a	Tender Batcave	1'26"
11m2b	Batsuit—Charge of the Batmobile	1'34"
	Prince: "Trust"	2'22"
12m2	Batwing I	16"
12m3	Batwing II (A)	3'45"
12m3c	Batwing II (B)	1'50"
13m1	Cathedral Chase	4'32"
13m2	Waltz	3'45"
13m3	Showdown A	1'10"
13m4	Showdown II	3'35"
14m2	Finale (revised)	1'34"
14m3	End Credits	1'16"
	Prince: "Scandalous"	2'22"

The musical text of *Batman* can be divided into several broad categories, which will be discussed in much greater detail in the final chapters. However, the principal types of music in the text are the thematic music of Elfman's score, derived from the five-note 'Bat-theme' (figure 4.1); whole-tone music, which is also a prominent feature of the score; and the various pieces of music that the Joker appears to appropriate for his own use. This category includes most of the diegetic music mentioned above that comes from sources other than Elfman's score, and some elements within the score, such as a Straussian waltz, and the pastiche easy-listening music used in his spoof commercial for lethal cosmetics.

Figure 4.1: The Bat-Theme
Danny Elfman, Batman *Score, "Titles," Bars 4–5*

These three main types of music are all very different. The Bat-theme is usually scored for full orchestra in a rich, classical Hollywood idiom that modulates frequently to unexpected keys and usually places melodies in the brass or low woodwind sections, and this is undoubtedly the music for which the score is best known. The whole-tone music tends to be more fragmented and is essentially gestural and textural rather than melodic, with more weight being given to higher woodwind, strings, and percussion. The Joker's appropriated music has no set instrumental identity although there are some definite orchestral tendencies: the easy-listening music favors strings, especially *pizzicato* strings; the Straussian waltz is again for full orchestra and also makes significant use of the cymbals, an instrument not noticeably used in other parts of the score. These tendencies also correspond to the observation that one of the identifying features of the Joker's music is the use of unusual timbres and textures, compared with the more orthodox timbres and classical sound of Batman's music.

Although all these different types of music are found in Elfman's score, it is quite easy to concentrate on the thematic music and overlook the second two categories because they are idiomatically not only different but, in the case of the Joker's music, they are obviously borrowed from other sources rather than composed from scratch by Elfman. Another reason why they might be overlooked is because the whole-tone music lacks an obvious melodic theme, while the Joker's music has no consistent theme. Very often, it is melody that lodges in the memory both during and after watching a film, with the result that music lacking an obvious melody is less likely to be recalled after the film has finished. Given that the score of *Batman* arguably only has one theme, this may affect how the score is perceived, recalled, and described after the event.

Although the score of *Batman* has several identifiable melodies, only the Bat-theme can truly be regarded as a theme. Batman has several different motifs associated with him, but all of them are directly related to fragments and variations of his main theme. The melodies of the Joker's various pieces of music act as musical objects rather than as themes: they remain self-contained and static and are used in a small number of very specific episodes. Some of them, such as the Prince songs and the melody of "Joker's Commercial," are used only once, and the melodies used on more than one occasion generally retain their original melodic identity and are not subjected to the thoroughgoing processes of variation and transformation through which the Bat-theme is put. The dominance of the Bat-theme in the audience's memory is also made much more likely by the fact that many of the accompaniment motifs throughout the score are also derived from fragments, variations, and inversions of it. The various ostinato figures in cues such as "Shootout" and "Clown Attack" are connected to the Bat-theme in the types of patterns and intervals that predominate, and in the use of minor-key tonalities, while the frequent arpeggio-style accompaniments and countermotifs also occupy the Bat-theme's sound world: many of the arpeggiated string figures have added sixths, recalling both the minor triad and the minor sixth within the Bat-theme.

Elfman's approach to film scoring has a strong resemblance to classical film scoring because of the musical idiom and forces he uses. The most memorable, thematically driven cues in the score are written on a grand orchestral scale with harps, organ, choir, a wide range of percussion, and a large brass section—six horns, four trumpets, four trombones, and two tubas. His musical idiom in this film clearly harks back to Wagner and Mahler via the Hollywood Golden Age composers such as Korngold and Waxman. It was through composers such as these that Wagnerian ideas found their way into film scoring practice. The processes whereby music provides a psychological dimension to the film, communicating to us what the characters are thinking and feeling, can be traced to the techniques Wagner used to achieve this same aim in his operas, particularly leitmotif. This kind of thinking informed the Golden Age composers in the way the music that they wrote for film functioned, and it continues to be the function that music is most associated with in film. Film music interprets and describes what we see on-screen: it locates a film emotionally, and often geographically and historically; it indicates point of view, identifies the roles and functions of characters, while on a more pragmatic level it also paces action and provides continuity, "carr[ying] the spectator over the rough spots of the diegesis."[5]

In terms of the function of Elfman's music, although the musical idiom is similar to that of the Golden Age composers, he is often working in a significantly different way. First, there are very few instances in which he uses music to locate a film in either time or place. The closest he comes to this is in his two historical films, *Sommersby* and *Black Beauty*, with the use of a guitar in the former and pipe and fiddle in the latter. In *Mars Attacks!* he uses the theremin to 'locate' the film in 1950s' science fiction, but this is a self-referential cinematic ploy and quite different from the historical and geographical conventions of the classical cinema, conventions that are still adhered to in many modern film scores. His use of a late-romantic orchestral idiom in *Batman* effectively renders the music timeless: this is classical film scoring's 'default idiom,' used for music that is not intended to evoke a specific time or place, despite the fact that it could logically evoke nineteenth-century Germany. If anything, in *Batman* it evokes classical Hollywood scoring and with it, a particular type of heroic narrative.

Elfman uses *Batman*'s music to create momentum, pace action, and to create continuity between scenes and shots, much as would be expected in a classical film score. The score also uses music to underline the unseen or psychological implications of scenes, particularly in relation to ideas of conflict within characters, but this is done in a very subtle and complex way and is an example of a clear difference between the idiom and technique of classical scoring practice and Elfman's practice. Elfman's harmonic idiom may seem Wagnerian but his use of music to underline the unseen implications of scenes is not, an effect of the essentially monothematic score. Wagner, like the classical Hollywood composers, used themes to bring unseen ideas, objects, or people into a scene musically. In a score that only has one major character identified by theme, this becomes more difficult: Batman has the Bat-theme and the Joker adopts his own musical strategy by appropriating a whole range of themes for himself out of the music available, but Vicki and the secondary characters are thematically unrepresented. As the leitmotivic approach is effectively impossible, Elfman uses different strategies such as changes in modality and meter as his principal techniques to achieve a comparable result. In particular, he uses triple time in contrast to duple time, major key in contrast to minor key, and the whole-tone scale in opposition to the romantic harmonic idiom, these musical ideas being used to create and underline the sense of duality both within Bruce-Batman's character and in his relationship with the Joker.

There is also practically no mickey-mousing in the score, another generally accepted technique of classical film scoring. While the music does respond to and pace the action, it avoids the obvious mimicking of physical gestures with musical ones. For example, in the opening scene of the film, as the family approaches a corner in the back alley, the music builds in tension, anticipating the attack of the mugger waiting unseen on the other side. As he appears around the corner and hits the father with the butt of his gun, the music does not parallel this with a musical gesture, which might have been a fairly obvious 'hit-point' for music and action to coincide. Likewise, there is a similarly obvious hit-point near the end of the film where the Joker, dancing with Vicki, pretends to shoot himself with a toy gun—again, the music makes no attempt to imitate this gesture. Other obvious stock-in-trade gestures of the classical score—ascending and descending passages that imitate ascending or descending movement—are also entirely absent from the score. The brief "Up Building" cue, for example, where the camera rushes up the side of a skyscraper to Grissom's office, is largely characterized by a rapid descending motif in strings and woodwind: the score captures the sense of pace the shot requires but refrains from obvious imitation of the movement in the scene. This is something that can also be observed at the various points when people and objects fall from great heights: as a general rule, the pitch of the music tends either to remain static or to travel in the opposite direction to the movement.

Again, this is a feature of Elfman's scoring that, while not typical of Golden Age scoring, reflects the specific influence of Herrmann, who tended "to avoid close synchronization with on-screen events" in his scores.[6] Elfman's score is often highly gestural, with musical motives and textures that correspond to ideas of movement and the body, but those gestures tend to correspond to ideas of tone more than visual action. The cue "Jack vs. Ekhart," where Napier meets the corrupt policeman in a back alley early in the film, is a case in point: the thudding of the low piano note evokes the thudding of the heart, a musical gesture that metaphorically describes the danger and tension between the characters rather than illustrating the on-screen action. One of the rare, unequivocal moments of mickey-mousing is after Batman and Vicki fall from the cathedral and end up dangling gently from a cable: as they sway back and forth, the music rocks gently with them.

Elfman has used the standard idiom but not the standard techniques of classical scoring. He has replaced the multiple themes of many classical scores with a single theme in the standard idiom. This is set alongside a range of pastiche and borrowed musics used for the Joker in quite different idioms and, although these are part of his score, they seem quite separate and distinct from it. However, the fact that only the thematic material appears in the 'Wagner by way of Korngold' idiom makes the classical idiom of the score appear deceptively overwhelming. K. J. Donnelly believes that the *Batman* score "takes the techniques of the classical film score and elevate[s] them to the level of cliché,"[7] but arguably it is more a case that Elfman takes the *idiom* of the classical film score, and it is his marginalization of classical techniques that results in a score that might superficially seem to be a parody of the classical style. It is less because of the elements of classical technique that have been exaggerated and more because of the elements that have been omitted that the score seems, in Donnelly's view, to lack subtlety.[8] If one tries to read *Batman's* music solely in the context of classical techniques, Elfman might well seem to have oversimplified and exaggerated these to the point of parody: taking the idea of leitmotivic character-identification and then only having one leitmotif, reused *ad infinitum*; giving the sentimental arrangement of "Beautiful Dreamer" to the homicidal Joker as his love theme; and juxtaposing the exuberance of the Straussian waltz with scenes of violence and murder. However, in the case of the

Joker's music, the sense of musical parody is entirely intentional, and it was Burton himself who asked for these two pieces to be included in the score as an important aspect of how the film overall constructs and positions that character;[9] and in the case of the music written for Batman and Bruce, it is the idiom rather than the techniques that are derived most clearly from classical film scoring.

Scoring the Superhero

The scoring of superheroes was firmly established in the late 1970s and early 1980s by John Williams, who scored all of the cinematic superhero films discussed in chapter 3, the *Star Wars* and *Indiana Jones* trilogies and the *Superman* quartet. Jeff Bond has observed that the main title themes for *Star Wars* and *Superman* are structural duplicates, and even a brief examination of them proves his point admirably.[10] The first obvious common characteristic of the two themes is that they are major key marches that give the principal melody to the brass section. Both start with a fanfarelike introduction followed by a bold statement of the main theme from the brass section punctuated by timpani and accompanied by a syncopated rhythmic ostinato from low brass and strings. The *Superman* main title is about three times as long as that of *Star Wars*, which comes in at a bare eighty seconds, but this is due largely to the fact that whereas *Superman* has a long opening credit sequence, all three films of the first *Star Wars* trilogy open with an on-screen update of the story so far, a direct evocation of the superhero cinema serials of the 1940s. The main title gives only this episode information and none of the usual opening credits, resulting in its unusual brevity.

The melodic and rhythmic outline of these two very famous themes is also remarkably similar. Both start with a triplet upbeat, followed by a tonic-to-dominant open fifth and a falling triplet figure. Both end with a repeating phrase consisting of a triplet and a repeating figure of an upward leap and a descent back to the dominant.

What gives them their heroic character is largely the harmonic stability created by the use of tonic-dominant intervals and the energetic character of their march rhythms. The punchy, confident, militaristic orchestration of *Star Wars* and *Superman* results in the sense of action and optimism that is central to their main characters. This is further enhanced by the absolute regularity of the rhythmic treatment. The use of triplets and dotted figures prevents the march rhythm from becoming too monotonous, but other than brief hemiolas between sections in *Superman*, the march rhythm is constant, and even the hemiolas do not disrupt the basic pulse. *Star Wars* is the slower at around MM112 with *Superman* at a brisk MM120.

These heroic themes, then, are major key, up-tempo, and largely devoid of chromaticism that might undermine the stability of the tonal center, musical metaphors for the largely uncomplicated, optimistic, and energetic heroes to whom they belong. The *Indiana Jones* theme, while being more different melodically, bears the same structural characteristics as its two predecessors, one of the main differences being that it replaces the triplet motif with a dotted rhythmic figure.[11]

Superficially, Elfman's main title for *Batman* adheres to the dramatic, quasi-militaristic sound of Williams's scoring. However, one of the features most regularly commented on in relation to Elfman's scoring—and the *Batman* theme in particular—is the idea of the 'darkness' of the music. Despite the superficial resemblances, Elfman's approach to scoring his superhero is altogether different from Williams's, reflecting the differences in Batman's character discussed in chapter 3. The most obvious contrast is that his theme is in a minor key and it is not actually a march, although it could be mistaken for one. The opening fanfare of Williams's themes is replaced here by a slow, canonic unwinding of the Bat-theme, with the tempo at MM70, which is far too slow for a march. At the end of this introductory section, as the theme enters in a more obviously militaristic manner, the pulse more than doubles to MM146, which is more of a gallop than a march. In fact, the Bat-theme is treated in a more varied manner than any of Williams's superhero themes, the change of tempo being one aspect of this. Batman is not a simple, open character, and the open fifths, straightforward march rhythms, and diatonic clarity of Williams's themes—which describe his heroes so well—would have been entirely inappropriate here. Batman has problems: as discussed earlier, he is a deeply troubled and traumatized individual and, just as he is positioned somewhat flexibly between the opposing powers of crime and the law, so his music is also 'flexible,' both harmonically and rhythmically. Throughout the score, the most distinctive and memorable aspects of the sound of Elfman's music—and the key features of his 'gothic' style—are the almost constant melodic variations that cause sudden harmonic slips into unexpected keys, the regular reinvention of the rhythmic shape of the basic theme, the minor tonality, and orchestration that generally gives the theme itself to brass instruments and bassoon.

The *Batman Motion Picture Soundtrack*

Elfman is, quite famously, not the only musician who wrote music for Burton's *Batman*, and it is quite possible that Prince was expecting to supply the whole musical soundtrack: he visited the set while the film was in production and, on seeing Anton Furst's Gotham City, reportedly said "I can hear the music."[12] This is an almost identical reaction to that of Elfman, who also visited the set during filming and, in numerous interviews, has attributed the inspiration for the *Batman* theme to the visual impact of the set.[13]

Prince's *Batman* album is a coherent and self-contained song cycle that stands alongside Burton's film and intersects it at numerous points.[14] The appeal of writing music for the film to Prince is clear: he had been involved with the film industry before, with his fantasy-musical autobiography *Purple Rain* (1984), and the narrative of *Batman* is clearly one that has parallels in the way he has constructed his own artistic persona. *Batman* is a film that explores the dualities of the characters of both Bruce-Batman and Jack-Joker, and positions them as each other's alter ego, one deeply moral and attempting to serve the greater good, the other driven by greed, insanity, and self-interest. Prince has long been exploring ideas of duality in his own music. His star sign is Gemini and his alter ego, a character named Gemini, appears in many of his songs as his 'evil twin.' Likewise, he has a second alter ego, Camille, who allows him to explore a male-female duality in parallel to the good-evil duality of Prince-Gemini. Gemini appears as an additional cast member in Prince's *Batman* songs, setting the Batman-Joker opposition against his own Prince-Gemini construction. One could extend his reasons for being interested in the film's narrative to his well-known love of the color purple, and the coincidence of that and the Joker's similar predilection for the color.

Royal Brown talks of pop music videos operating as miniversions of the films from which they emerge, but Prince's *Batman* album is, in a very real sense, a miniature version of Burton's film.[15] The eight songs follow a similar chronology to the film, a feature that is enhanced by the insertion of dialogue from the film at the start and end of some tracks, and each of the songs designates one or more of the film's central characters as its 'lead vocalist,' although all the songs are mainly sung by Prince himself. The result is not unlike a miniature rock-opera version of the film that largely supports Burton's positioning of the central characters, although Prince's reading of the tone of the film is very different from Elfman's. It is undoubtedly much more successful as an album than it would have been as the film soundtrack, where the demands of the dialogue and narrative are unlikely to have provided the lyrics with the amount of foregrounding they would have needed to be heard.

"The Future" occupies first place on the album and is also the first song to be heard in the film. Here, only the lyric "I've seen the future" is clearly audible, although we do we hear the words "the future" several times. It is an intriguing juxtaposition of lyric and image at the start of the film, if only because the opening shots of Gotham look far more like the past, with many of the on-screen characters dressed as if they are in the 1930s. From the outset, then, the soundtrack is reinforcing the temporal ambiguity that Burton and his designers Anton Furst and Bob Ringwood have created visually. The juxtaposition of Elfman's classical score and Prince's pop songs might also be seen as another aspect of that temporal ambiguity: the first two pieces of music in the film are Elfman's lushly romantic "Titles" for full orchestra, immediately followed by the drums and synthesizers of "The Future," so emphasizing the musical contrasts at a structural level.

Three of the songs on the album are 'sung' by the Joker—"Electric Chair," "Partyman," and "Trust"—and all of these are used in the film, either wholly or in part. Four songs are written about Vicki and Bruce-Batman's relationship. In "The Arms of Orion," Sheena Easton sings Vicki to Prince's Bruce in a song, which, in the chronology of the film, corresponds to Vicki and Bruce's romantic dinner and first night together. "Lemon Crush," sung by Vicki, balances "Vicki Waiting," sung by Bruce about his inability to commit to her. Where the latter is about Bruce not being ready, "Lemon Crush" is explicitly about the fact that Vicki is. This sequence of songs is concluded with "Scandalous," sung by Batman. Bruce's vacillation has been forgotten and Batman takes matters with Vicki into his own hands. The lyrics of "Vicki Waiting," "Lemon Crush," and "Scandalous" are all explicitly sexual in a way the film is not, and this is possibly one of the reasons why the songs, especially the quartet of songs relating to Vicki and Bruce-Batman, are largely absent from the film. Anwar Brett has commented that the relationship of the film's romantic couple is "highly sanitized and hygienic, more than you might expect from a journalist and a guy who dresses up as a glorified rodent for kicks," and this is a pattern common to Burton's other films.[16] There is not a single sex scene in any one of his films to date and the shot of Bruce and Vicki in bed together, where Vicki is already asleep, is the closest that Burton gets to putting an adult sexual relationship on-screen in his films. "The Arms of Orion" is as sexually inexplicit as Burton's love scene in the film, but Prince's other songs for the couple use a language and imagery that are unique to Prince's vision and quite different from the film that Burton actually made.

Donnelly describes Prince's songs as "an extension of the text beyond its traditional boundaries to include intersecting aesthetic products."[17] These intersections are manifested in the lyrics of the songs as much as in the songs' presence in the film itself. On the album, the fact that several of the songs contain sections of dialogue taken from the film soundtrack produces a reversal of the usual relationship of a film and the music written for it, the film now having been edited into the song. "Batdance" mixes lines of dialogue delivered by the Joker, Bruce, Batman, and Vicki; lyrics sung by both Gemini and Prince; quotations from other songs on the album ("Electric Chair" and "The Future"); and an instantly recognizable rearrangement of Neil Hefti's theme from the 1960s *Batman* television series. Given that "Batdance" was released before the film, it "provides an interface with the past, announcing the new *Batman* film through referencing the chorus vocals from . . . the camp 1960s television show [and providing] a musical bridge between the previous representation of the character and the oncoming film."[18] In fact, the only notable omission from "Batdance" is any reference to Elfman's music: instead, Prince's integration of his music, the Hefti theme, and the film's dialogue appears to locate the sound of the film firmly in the sphere of pop, creating a virtual version of *Batman* in which Prince's soundtrack is predominant and *Batman*'s own musical past exists on the fringes, but where his musical future is, ironically, nowhere to be heard.

The one clear point where Prince's music intersects with Elfman's score is in a motif Elfman uses that is taken from Prince's song "Scandalous." Superficially, the use of this material might seem an odd choice: it comes directly from one of the songs associated with Bruce and Vicki's relationship but the motif is not the melody sung by Prince but the accompaniment, which repeats this motif as a steady ostinato under the more improvisatory vocal line. This motif acts as the type of secondary theme often found in Elfman's otherwise monothematic scores, as outlined in chapter 2, although it has a quite specific relationship with the Bat-theme that will be discussed more fully in the next chapter.

The motif from Prince's "Scandalous" is positioned within *Batman* in a similar way to the melody of "(Everything I do) I do it for you" in *Robin Hood: Prince of Thieves* (1991). In both cases, the theme from a pop song written specifically for the film is then used in the score prior to the song's appearance in the end credits. The "Scandalous" motif occurs only in scenes involving Vicki Vale, and at first glance this indicates that it falls into exactly the same pattern as in films such as *Robin Hood* and *Highlander* (1983), where the pop song theme becomes a love theme associated with the principal female characters. In *Batman*, however, the "Scandalous" motif is not Vicki's theme. It does not represent her point of view: rather, as will be discussed further in chapter 5, it represents Bruce Wayne's point of view and his thoughts and feelings about her. Batman—rather than either Vicki or Bruce—is Prince's designated lead vocalist for this song on the album, although the theme is primarily used in scenes involving Vicki with Bruce rather than in scenes between Vicki and Batman or any other character.

Music and Silence

Unlike the resoundingly successful Bryan Adams song from *Robin Hood*—which broke records with the length of its stay in the number one position of the U.K. charts—"Scandalous" is far less well known away from the film or the album. "Batdance," not in the film, was the most successful single released from the album and was released before the film, reaching number one in the U.S. pop charts and number two in the United Kingdom; "Partyman," the song used for the Joker's museum scene, was the next most successful, reaching number eighteen in the United States pop charts and number fourteen in the United Kingdom. "Arms of Orion," also not in the film, made it into the top thirty in the United Kingdom but only reached number thirty-two in the United States; while "Scandalous" did not appear in the pop charts of either country, although it did get to number five in the less wide-reaching R&B charts. Nonetheless, "Scandalous" might have achieved what "(Everything I do) I do it for you" aimed for: placing the theme from the song within the film so that when the song appears in the end credits, the theme is instantly recognizable.

This certainly appears to have been the original intention, but the realization proves to be somewhat different. In the text of Elfman's completed score, there are a total of ten cues that use the "Scandalous" motif as a Love theme, although most of these are extremely brief. This situation is then amplified by several cuts that were made to Elfman's score that entirely removed two particularly significant Love theme cues, and the absence of music in these scenes highlights the very specific use of musical silence in particular situations and environments within the film.

Of the seven Love theme cues in the written score where the motif is the main material, five are concentrated into a ten-minute sequence half an hour into the film. They comprise the untitled, brief segue that takes Vicki and Bruce from the formal dining room to the kitchen, "Kitchen Dinner," "Stair Kiss," "Beddy Bye," and "Morning After." The theme's next appearance is in "The Truth," some thirty-five minutes later in the film, in the scene in Vicki's apartment when Bruce attempts to tell her he is Batman; and it is heard again approximately fifteen minutes after this in "Tender Batcave," after Vicki has finally learned the truth. The Love theme is also hinted at, although not actually stated, in "Bruce Contemplates" and "Showdown II," and its tenth and final appearance is embedded within a final transformation of the Bat-theme in "Finale" (see table 4.2).

Table 4.2: Overview of the Love Theme

Cue No.	Cue Title	Love Theme Use
4m3	Untitled (Segue)	single statement
4m3a	Kitchen Dinner	single statement
5m1a	Stair Kiss	single statement
5m3	Beddy Bye	variation and transformation alongside Bat-theme
5m4	Morning After	several statements
7m1	Bruce Contemplates	texture and orchestration used rather than theme
10m1	The Truth	several statements
11m2a	Tender Batcave	several statements
13m4	Showdown II	accompaniment only in section toward end of cue
14m2	Finale (revised)	multiple variations and transformations alongside Bat-theme
	Prince: "Scandalous"	accompaniment motif, multiple statements

Of these cues, the two that are missing from the final film are "Morning After" and "The Truth." "Morning After" is the cue, which contains the clearest and most extended statements of the Love theme up to this point. Omitting it leaves the theme somewhat underrepresented in the remaining music. It is given only a single, partial statement in the segue and another single statement at the end of "Kitchen Dinner," which is mainly based on the underlying chordal accompaniment rather than the motif itself. It has another single statement in "Stair Kiss," which is also very brief; and "Beddy Bye" contains disguised and partial statements of the Love theme, transforming it back into the Bat-theme. The omission of "Morning After" effectively robs the score of the ability to establish the "Scandalous" motif firmly as the theme hinted at in the preceding cues. This is then further complicated by the omission of "The Truth," which would have been another complete and unambiguous exploration of the Love theme. Therefore, when it does finally appear again in "Tender Batcave," the audience has not heard this theme clearly since its single, brief statement in "Stair Kiss" fifty-five minutes previously. The absence of "Morning After" and "The Truth" seriously undermines the ability of this theme to establish itself and its narrative significance in the audience's memory.

There are some sound dramatic reasons for the removal of these two cues. Both were to have been within scenes that are profoundly uncomfortable for Bruce. The first is the morning after his night with Vicki, at which point he is having serious doubts as to whether this is a relationship he can pursue, making a series of excuses to her about why he cannot fix a date to see her again; the second scene is where he is attempting to tell her the most profound and peculiar secret of his life. To set these scenes to music, and music designed to act as a romantic counterbalance to the drama of the Bat-theme itself, would make these scenes much less uncomfortable and much more gentle: and in so doing, they would probably make Bruce's desire for a relationship with Vicki seem less problematic for him. The removal of the music renders the scenes cold and awkward, revealing the silence between his lines and Vicki's, the silence that Eisler and Adorno identified as one of the primary reasons for having music in films in the first place.[19] However, the fact remains that the Love theme is unable to establish itself within the sound of the score in the way that Elfman originally intended and, although the silence in these scenes undoubtedly enhances the film's narrative overall, it is possible that Elfman would have given the theme greater weight earlier in the film if he had known in advance that these two cues were to be omitted.

Another effect of these cuts is to alter the impact of Bruce as a character within the film. By removing much of Bruce's underscoring, in particular the theme that distinguishes him from Batman, the extent to which the audience will identify with him as a central character is lessened and the extent to which attention is focused on Batman is increased. In many ways, this is only natural: the film, after all, is not called *Bruce Wayne*. Yet if one compares how much screen time each side of the character has, Batman is only on-screen for about four minutes in the first hour of the film, whereas Bruce is on-screen for close to fifteen; and Bruce has some fifty lines of dialogue during this time to Batman's meager four.[20] In the second hour of the film, Batman is on-screen for almost half of it, compared to Bruce's ten minutes, but this still means that overall, Bruce is only on-screen for six minutes less than Batman in the course of the film. He also has another thirty lines of dialogue, whereas Batman manages just nineteen lines in twenty-seven minutes, and many of these are short and monosyllabic utterances such as "hold on," "get in the car," "let's go," and "how much do you weigh?" Bruce Wayne is clearly not the world's most articulate man, especially in comparison to the positively garrulous Joker, but he still manages to outtalk Batman by a considerable amount. Bruce's sonic identity is, therefore, largely formed in his dialogue, the sound of his voice and his characteristic hesitations, while Batman's sonic identity—in the general absence of dialogue—is almost entirely constructed in his music. It is, at least in part, the music that makes Batman seem the more central character. Although this may not have been the original intention of director or composer, the dominance of Batman in the second half of the film is effectively prepared by the fact that Bruce is not allowed to establish a strongly competing musical identity in the first half. Bruce is effectively subsumed by the Bat-theme into the wider Batman identity, a process completed by Bruce's absence from the last quarter of the film.

The fact that the Love theme 'belongs' to Bruce and not Vicki is further emphasized by the fact that in her two other main environments, the newsroom and her apartment, there is generally no music, the exception being the music that the Joker brings with him when he comes to visit her at home. None of the newsroom scenes have any music except when Vicki and Knox are looking at microfiche images of Bruce as a child after his parents' murder, which produces the Bat-theme in the underscore. The Joker and Batman both take their music with them wherever they go, but the result is that when they are absent, so is the music unless some specific object or idea—such as the old newspaper photographs—invokes their musical image within the scene.

There are also two other cues omitted from Elfman's score that represent a conscious and fairly late decision on Burton's behalf to introduce silence into the film. "Board Meeting" was to have accompanied the Joker's opening speech to the board of assembled mobsters following Grissom's murder: removing Elfman's fast, percussive, and chromatic music makes the Joker appear more rational and in control. The scene is almost unnaturally still in contrast to the excessive movement that has been associated with the Joker in his two preceding scenes, the "Surgery" scene and Grissom's circus-clowning murder. Although we cannot in fact see the Joker, we can hear his voice, which sounds relatively normal, lower in pitch, and with the hysterical giggling of the previous scenes replaced by a breathy chuckle. The rhythmically erratic music of the intended cue might well have made him appear considerably more unhinged during this speech, in turn lessening the impact of his unexpectedly bizarre murder-by-handbuzzer of the hapless Anton a scant thirty seconds after the cue was due to have finished. The absence of music reflects the extent to which the Joker is attempting to appear normal. Jack Napier, like all the other characters, has no music or theme of his own, but the Joker appears to have a great deal of diegetic control over his music in the film. The absence of music at this point might even be read as him suppressing it himself, in order to sound more like Jack.

A very brief cue was also written to follow Alfred's line to Bruce in the Batcave toward the end of the film: "I have no wish to fill my few remaining years grieving for the loss of old friends . . . or their sons." The cue entitled ". . . Or their sons" was to have been played as Bruce watches Alfred leave and consists of a single statement of the Bat-theme played very softly by low, muted strings, accompanied by timpani, a mournful, brooding reminder of the fact that it is being Batman that threatens Bruce's life and threatens to leave Alfred mourning him. Removing the cue leaves Bruce watching Alfred leave but without invoking the musical image of Batman. Instead, there is simply silence, the visual and aural image of Bruce in complete isolation, an image that would not be possible if the music were metaphorically to bring Batman into the picture.

Music and Characterization

One of the objections that has been made about the use of popular music in film is that it "robs the film of musical unity, which the traditional leitmotif structure and other considerations of a well-composed score guarantee."[21] However, in *Batman* the lack of unity between the idiom of the orchestral score and that of Prince's songs contributes significantly to the construction of the narrative, creating a specifically musically distinction between Batman and the Joker. The only uses of songs by Prince within the diegesis of the film that are not identified with the Joker are the three largely inaudible songs at the start of the film, "The Future," "Vicki Waiting," and "Electric Chair," all of which occur before the Joker has been created. In the latter two songs, Prince's voice has been removed from the soundtrack, rendering the music that is left both hard to hear and practically impossible to identify as being by Prince; and as noted above, the clearest lyric heard from the first song is "the future." In the context of the film's use of Prince's songs, this can be read as a premonitory reference to either Batman or the Joker himself: the song is given to Batman on Prince's album, but Prince's songs later become the Joker's preserve.

The museum scene and the festival parade are the only two scenes where Prince's music is foregrounded, both of them scenes that center on the Joker in pursuit of his destructive and homicidal art, clearly establishing Prince and his songs as belonging to the Joker's musical identity. This is in stark idiomatic contrast to the romantic orchestral writing of Elfman's score that identifies Batman. The effect of these two types of music upon the audience is very different, not just because of the different musical idiom and instrumental forces, but because of the presence of words and of Prince's distinctive voice in the songs. As Gorbman observes, the lyrics of a song do not operate in the audience's "perceptual background" in the same way that the music of a film score often does. "The presence of words being sung automatically makes us attend to them," with the songs demanding our attention in tandem with the action and taking the place of dialogue in the sonic foreground.[22] They are also clearly woven into the narrative: in "Partyman," the lyrics refer to the colors red and green, the same colors being used by the Joker to 'improve the paintings;' while in the festival parade scene, as Prince's song "Trust" finishes, the Joker asks the crowd "who do you trust?"

The meanings and narrative positions generated by the different musics of Batman and the Joker reflect the way in which the use of scoring and songs in film soundtracks generates different types of audience identification with characters. Classical Hollywood scoring, to which Elfman's Bat-theme scoring undoubtedly belongs idiomatically, generates what Anahid Kassabian has described as 'assimilating identifications' that encourage the audience, regardless of their age, gender, race, or sexual orientation to identify with the hero of the piece who, in the vast majority of films, is white, male, and heterosexual. Conversely, popular music encourages 'affiliating' identifications: our response to different types of popular music is more likely to be affected by such things as our age, gender, race, and sexual orientation, and the way characters are associated with popular music will therefore affect how individual members of an audience will perceive and respond to them.[23]

Batman has both types of music coexisting but, given that one of the central themes of the film is the sense of duality between Batman and the Joker, even though Batman is technically the hero, they have an equal status and compete for centrality. Depending on how individual members of the audience feel about Prince and his music, there will probably be a quite diverse range of attitudes toward and opinions of the Joker: Jonathan Rosenbaum found himself "preferring the creativity and vitality of Jack/Joker" to the "humorless, iconographic rigidity" of Batman,[24] whereas other members of the audience, particularly those less enamored of Prince's music, are more likely to be assimilated into an identification of Batman as the more credible protagonist.

In fact, the Joker's identification with the popular music in the film also supports Kassabian's observation that popular music is often used in relation to characters who are not white, heterosexual heroes, and that films with unconventional heroes—women, black men, gay men—are more likely to have scores compiled from popular music than orchestral scores. As Andrew Ross has noted in his critique of the racial subtext of the *Batman* narrative, the Joker is covertly coded as a black character. He "plays his role in *whiteface*, and sports an involuntary rictus grin that caricatures, along with his new, pathologically delirious personality, the old minstrel blackface routine of putting on a happy face."[25] His association with popular music in the soundtrack—especially the music of a black artist—reinforces his position in opposition to Batman (who completes the black-white inversion by wearing a black mask) and his orchestral music.

Although the Joker is not the hero of this film, his identification with popular music means that he, unlike Bruce, can never simply be subsumed into Batman's musical identity. Having his own collection of musical objects—rather than simply having his own musical theme within what is otherwise Batman's score—makes him a subversive musical presence within the film. He cannot be absorbed into the orchestral score: instead, part of Batman's triumph is his own appropriation of the Joker's music. As will be discussed in the following chapter, their final, physical battle is underpinned by a musical battle for melodic dominance. Similarly, the fact that the final Prince song, "Scandalous" appears in the end credits as Bruce-Batman's song, with the Love theme embedded in its accompaniment, represents the final defeat of the Joker, the negation of his distinctive musical voice.

Synergy and the Reception of *Batman*

Batman is cited by Jeff Smith as a demonstration of 'synergy' at work in film, a term coined in the film industry in the early 1980s to describe the phenomenon of successful film and music cross-promotion.[26] Synergy is more an economic than an aesthetic phenomenon, the strategy that underlies the well-established diversification by major film studios into the recording industry, "a strategy that not only creates multiple profit centers but also serves to spread risk and maximize resources."[27] This economic strategy has aesthetic implications stemming from the resulting interaction of orchestral score and popular music both within the film's narrative and in the wider context of the public perception of the film's musical identity.

Among the best-known examples of synergy is *Robin Hood: Prince of Thieves*, where Bryan Adams's and Michael Kamen's song "(Everything I do) I do it for you" spent seven weeks at number one in the U.S. pop charts and fifteen weeks at number one in the United Kingdom in the months following the film's release. Although, like "Scandalous" in *Batman*, the song does not appear in the film until the end credits, it has been anticipated throughout the film by the use of the melody as Marion's theme, and so it is instantly recognizable when it appears at the end. The pop video for this song uses both scenes from the film and shots of Adams himself, filmed performing in similar locations. The cross-marketing of film and song was so successful that more than one person remembers, quite falsely, that the song occurs within the film's narrative rather than during the final credits.[28]

As Claudia Gorbman and K. J. Donnelly have both pointed out, the majority of writers examining film music up to the mid-1990s considered the use of popular song in film as problematic and even as an aberration, assuming they bothered to consider it at all.[29] Gorbman cites Royal S. Brown (1994) while Donnelly cites Kathryn Kalinak (1992) as emblematic of the tendency to ignore or otherwise dismiss the contribution of popular songs to film narratives.[30] Even Jeff Smith, whose *The Sounds of Commerce* generally presents a very positive reading of popular song's contribution to film, asserts that Prince's songs for *Batman* "function largely as a commercial tie-in," and does not view them as contributing to the narrative in a meaningful way, a role he ascribes entirely to Elfman's score.[31]

The aesthetic separation of Elfman's score and Prince's songs in terms of idiom and use within the film is compounded and highlighted in the marketing of the music, as both sets of compositions were released on separate albums. Prince's eight songs were released as the album, marketed as the *Batman Motion Picture Soundtrack* in advance of the film's release. "Batdance" was released as a single two weeks before the film and the album was issued three days before *Batman* went on general release. Elfman's soundtrack was originally only going to be represented by one or two tracks on Prince's album, but *Batman's* producer, Jon Peters, was sufficiently impressed with the score to allow it a separate release in August 1989.[32]

However, as pointed out above, despite the fact that the marketing process seemed to be giving far more emphasis to Prince's music than Elfman's, only six of the songs made it into the film in any form and of these, three appear in the diegetic background and are almost totally obscured by ambient sound and dialogue, while "Scandalous" is only heard after the narrative is completed. "Vicki Waiting" and "Electric Chair" are largely inaudible while "The Future" is reduced to around thirty seconds of music that is only momentarily audible as anything more than a drum track, appearing as if issuing from a store on Gotham's main street. These three songs last over thirteen minutes on the album; in the film, they take up less than four. In this light, it is hard to see how the release of Prince's album as the soundtrack album can really be justified, lending weight to the idea that the inclusion of the material was a largely commercial gesture, which had a fortunate effect on the narrative construction of the Joker. Prince, while certainly not purely motivated by commercial concerns but by a desire to be artistically involved in the project, might well have also been hoping that the publicity from the film would help revive his career following the relatively poor reception of his previous album, *Lovesexy* (1988).

The marketing decisions concerning the soundtrack must be attributed primarily to Warner Bros., and the somewhat deceptive promotion of Prince's album as the soundtrack reflects the fact that the marketing of the film as a whole was very aggressive, with a comprehensive campaign involving products ranging from action figures to a *Batman* breakfast cereal. As Burton reportedly commented to Elfman in the run-up to the film's release, "is there a movie here, or just something that goes along with the merchandising?"[33]

However, the involvement of Prince and his music is clearly not an entirely commercial gesture. The use of songs by a specific artist is repeated in Burton's early films, with songs by Harry Belafonte in *Beetlejuice* and Tom Jones in *Edward Scissorhands*; and these songs always act as an idiomatic counterpoint to Elfman's scores. To regard the inclusion of Prince's songs as a gesture of pure commercialism, therefore, is to do an injustice to both Prince and Burton. It is also quite evident that, in comparison to other areas of *Batman* merchandising, the marketing of the music as a way of promoting the film was actually rather less aggressive than was common at the time. *Saturday Night Fever* (1977) was preceded by the carefully timed release of four singles from its soundtrack in the four months prior to the film's own release, and this tactic was so successful that it became a model for other film and music cross-marketing strategies.[34] The growing awareness of film and music synergies is reflected in a *Billboard* article from 1979 that lists the elements required to create a successful soundtrack album: "commercially viable music. Timing. Film cooperation on advance planning and tie-ins. Music that's integral to the movie. A hit movie. A hit single. A big-name recording star. A big-name composer."[35] The only ingredient missing from the *Batman* mix is that at this point, Elfman was not a big-name composer, but his music did not appear on Prince's soundtrack album and all the other elements would have been firmly in place. This includes the requirement that the music be integral to the movie, despite the fact that so much of the album is actually absent from or suppressed in the final film: "Partyman," "Trust," and "Scandalous" are all, in their separate ways, essential to the narrative; and the narrative is, in turn, essential to "Batdance."

The sound of *Batman*'s score encodes the film's principal narrative ideas, in particular the various internal and external dualities of Batman himself and his relationships with Bruce and the Joker. Essentially, all the music in the film is positioned in relation to Batman—either it is his music or it is 'other,' belonging to the Joker and therefore threatening the privileging of Batman's position as victorious hero within the narrative. The steadily increasing aural dominance of the Bat-theme as the film progresses reaffirms his centrality, and his ultimate triumph over the Joker is simultaneously a defeat of his competing musical identity.

Chapter 5

Reading the Score: Part I

No reading of a film or its music can ever truly be complete, if only because there are as many potential readings as there are readers. The following analysis of the score of *Batman* aims, however, to be as inclusive as possible of different interpretations available from the aural and visual texts and chapters 5 and 6 follow two separate routes through the musical narrative. Although these readings of the music will frequently take a chronological approach in the way material is ordered, nonetheless many of the observations are dependent on knowing what happens later in the film and in the score. When Elfman started to write the music, he already knew what happened at the end of the film, and so must we in order to appreciate fully how he is structuring his material and how he is speaking to narrative ideas from the very first moments of the main title cue.

Film music at its best is always going to be wasted on cinema audiences to a certain extent: viewers may hear the music, but they rarely listen to it the first time they see a film, and many will never pay close attention to the music at all, no matter how many times they rewatch it. The composer, on the other hand, may well have spent hundreds of hours creating the score, interpreting the film's narrative and the director's intentions, and seeking to enhance these through the meanings embedded in the music.

The sophistication of a film score like *Batman* as a signifier of narrative meaning requires a depth of creative thought and a high level of conscious intent to create music that is meaningful within the cinematic context. Much of the following analysis is an attempt to unpick the thought processes that led Elfman to write the score in the way he did and to reveal the ways in which his music articulates the film's constructions of narrative and the positioning of its characters.

   This analysis rests simultaneously on both the score as it is heard
in the film and as it appears in the written text, where, on occasion,
additional readings are available that complement ideas communicated
by the aural text but which are only available from knowledge of how
the music has been notated. The score itself, as held in the Warner Bros.
Music Library in Los Angeles, is Steve Bartek's copy of his orchestration of Elfman's score. The score is 703 pages long, including unused
cues and alternate versions, most notably of the cue "Stair Kiss," which
exists in four different versions. There is also an alternate opening to
"Descent into Mystery," and ten pages of both manuscript and handwrit-
ten notes relating to alterations made to the main title cue.
   A noticeable feature of the notation is that Bartek (and presumably
Elfman) never uses key signatures, although this is itself not a unique
characteristic of Elfman's film scoring practice: Max Steiner, for example, also used key signatures relatively rarely.[1] The absence of key signatures in Elfman's score is often quite reasonable: much of the music is
atonal or whole tone, and when it is tonal, it often modulates rapidly to
diatonically distant keys. Omitting key signatures altogether and notat-
ing all sharps and flats as accidentals, although probably a consequence
of the informality of his musical training, is ultimately no more untidy
or confusing a way of dealing with the rapid shifting from one key area
to another. Another consequence of the omission of key signatures in
the score and Elfman's unorthodox musical background is that chords,
especially in nontonal passages and at points of modulation, are often
'badly spelt' in conventional musical terms, with sharps and flats being
mixed quite freely as one reads the score vertically; and similarly, chromatic melodies and motifs in otherwise tonal music tend to follow the
logic of the instrumental line more than the logic of the underlying key.
This will be seen variously in examples in the following two chapters:
figure 5.1 contains a $G\sharp$ in the key of C minor because, in the context of
the melodic line, this is actually more natural than the $A\flat$; less logically,
the passage shown in figure 5.6 is actually in unison, a fact concealed
by the fact that half the violins are playing $E\flat$ and the other half have $D\sharp$.
In the musical examples used in the following chapters, where the entire
example is unambiguously in one specific key, and sharps or flats have
been used consistently in Elfman's score, a key signature has been in-
serted. However, the more anomalous spellings have not been corrected
in that they are an aspect of how the score has been written that reflects
Elfman's own compositional process: on the horizontal axis, his writing
of individual instrumental lines tends to be very logical, and it is largely

the vertical structure that deviates from the accepted norms of musical notation. This is probably also a consequence of the fact that although he handwrites up to 50 percent of the score, he also uses sequencer printouts, and sequencers can produce this kind of inconsistent spelling of accidentals.[2]

The analytical route taken in chapter 6 examines the Bat-theme itself and the multiple meanings that Elfman generates from it and its variations. The route followed in this chapter traces the relationship between Batman and the Joker, examining how the music supports and creates ideas of duality and opposition between the two characters. Through his use of different types of musical material—tonal and whole-tone music, orchestral and popular idioms—Elfman brings out Batman's problematic similarities to the Joker. At the same time, he also creates a musical identification for Batman that is quite different from his archenemy's, and the scoring allows us to hear his moral dilemma and decision making about whether he will be a just warrior or a vigilante, a law unto himself.

Batman's Act Structure

Much of the analysis in these two final chapters is set within the context of the film's three-act structure, as this is an important part of the film's own narrative architecture, which Elfman's musical narrative reflects. There is no specific indication of where the acts start and end in the typescript of Hamm and Skaaren's screenplay, but there was a correspondence about the three-act structure of the film between Skaaren and Burton in September 1988, and a three-act structure is clearly apparent in the film itself.[3] Table 5.1 shows the musical cues and how they relate to the three acts.

As expected, the first act establishes the characters but also lays the groundwork for several situations that will need to be resolved to bring the narrative to a close. We are introduced to all the principal and secondary players: we meet Batman, then Bruce, and then learn that they are the same person; we meet Knox and Vicki, and learn that it is Knox's persistent inquisitiveness that is making the Batman story an issue of public interest. We meet Jack Napier and Grissom, and discover that Grissom knows of Jack's affair with Alicia, which prompts the setup at Axis chemicals that is supposed to lead to Jack's death. Instead, it leads to his first confrontation with Batman and results in his fall into

Table 5.1: Position of Cues within the Act Structure*

Act 1

Titles (short)	Card Snap
Family—1st Bat	Batzone
Roof Fight	Axis Setup
Jack vs. Ekhart	Shootout
Up Building	

Act 2

Untitled (Segue)	Alicia's Mask
Kitchen Dinner	Vicki Gets a Gift
Surgery	Alicia's Unmasking
Stair Kiss	Rescue
Face Off	Batmobile Chase
Beddy Bye	Street Fight
Morning After	*Vicki Hides*
Board Meeting	Descent into Mystery
Roasted Dude	Bat Cave
Vicki Spys	Paper Throw
Clown Attack	*The Truth*
Bruce Contemplates/Photos	Joker's Poem
Men at Work	Sad Pictures
Wild—TV News Theme	*". . . or their Sons"*
Joker's Commercial	Challenge/Dream
Paper Spin	Tender Batcave

Act 3

Batsuit—Charge of the Batmobile	Waltz
Joker Flies to Gotham	Showdown A
Batwing I	Showdown II
Batwing II (A)	Finale (revised)
Batwing II (B)	End Credits
Cathedral Chase	

*Italics indicate omitted cues.

a vat of chemicals. Act 1 ends with the Joker's transformed hand emerging from the dark waters of the river as tubular bells chime ominously of terrible things to come.

Act 2 then starts with the juxtaposition of two very different episodes of new beginnings for the main characters: Vicki and Bruce have dinner and end up in bed together, while Jack is reborn as the Joker and exacts his revenge on Grissom. Almost immediately, things start to go wrong for Bruce-Batman. During the cue "Beddy Bye," we find that Bruce is no longer in bed with Vicki but is instead hanging upside down from his Bat-frame, bringing the idea of his Batman identity into the scene as the reason for their current spatial and subsequent emotional distance. Meanwhile, the Joker is in Grissom's office, where he focuses on the newspaper headline "Winged Freak Terrorizes Gotham Gangland," immediately giving him a new focus for his ambitions now that Grissom is out of the way. He proceeds to take over Grissom's empire and to explore his homicidal art, and he also encounters Vicki. This brings him into conflict with both Batman and Bruce, and in turn creates the reason why Vicki first meets Batman, when he comes to rescue her from the museum. However, by the end of this act, several important plot elements have been clarified and the seeds of resolution for the romantic side of the plot have been sown. Bruce attempts to tell Vicki the truth, although in the end it is Alfred who sees to this; and Bruce learns that it was Jack who killed his parents, giving him the emotional push he needs in order to confront the Joker in the final act. Act 2 ends with Bruce agreeing that he would like to try and make his relationship with Vicki work but that it will have to wait until the other side of Act 2's problems has been resolved and the Joker is defeated.

Act 3 is the extended final confrontation between Batman and the Joker. Initially it appears that the Joker has won: he shoots the Bat-plane out of the sky and kidnaps Vicki, taking her to the top of the cathedral where his helicopter will arrive shortly to collect him and take him to safety. Batman staggers from the wreckage of the Bat-plane and, clearly injured or at least concussed, he follows the Joker up the cathedral. After a series of reversals of fortune, the Joker is defeated, Vicki ends up in the arms of Bruce-Batman, and he finds a new role for himself as Gotham's protector, working with the law rather than separately from it.

Batman versus the Joker: A Musical Narrative

The narrative of *Batman* makes much of both the similarities and differences between the protagonist and antagonist. As outlined in chapter 3, they are positioned as being two sides of the same coin, with their traumatic origins, their split identities, and also with the mirroring of their associates: Vicki doubles Alicia as the love interest, Alfred doubles Bob the Goon as the faithful retainer, and Commissioner Gordon doubles Grissom as the figure of paternal authority. However, the differences between them are equally important: Batman retains his identity as Bruce, while the Joker loses his ability to be Jack; the Joker kills all three of his associates in the course of the film, while Batman forges new, stronger relationships with his. The Joker's trajectory is a rapid descent into the irrational; Batman's is one of reaching a healthier and less detached accommodation with the rest of the world through Vicki and Commissioner Gordon. He finds a workable place in society through love on the one hand and public service on the other.

Establishing Identities: Duality and Opposition in the Music of Act 1.

The first character to be established in the film is, unsurprisingly, Batman. As the eponymous hero of the film, Batman's musical identity is established by the main title cue, an identification of Batman and the Bat-theme (see figure 4.1) reinforced by the pairing of the theme with the initial sightings of him in the opening scene. The key elements of his identity are the theme itself and also the sound world it occupies: full orchestra, a minor-key tonality, and particular emphasis on the brass section and lower woodwind as the main carriers of the melody.

Although the Joker only comes into existence in the final moments of act 1, Jack Napier is very much in evidence throughout this act, and the Joker inherits several aspects of his musical identity. The first time we see him is with Alicia as he listens to District Attorney Harvey Dent's press conference speech on the radio, and there is no music at all in this scene. Batman was announced musically before we set eyes on him, his theme reiterated on his subsequent sightings, but Jack's introduction establishes no musical identity—one could even read this as establishing the absence of a musical identity, in particular, the absence of a theme.

We next see him in the back alley where he meets Eckhardt, the corrupt police officer. The cue before this is "Roof Fight," a cue written for Batman's fight with the muggers. "Roof Fight" uses one of Elfman's pre-laid synthesizer tracks, with several sections written in the whole-tone mode. This next cue, "Jack vs. Ekhart," (*sic*) also uses a pre-laid synthesizer track and is written entirely in the whole-tone mode, creating a musical connection between the "Roof Fight" confrontation of Batman and the muggers, and the confrontation of Jack and Eckhardt. At this point in the film, Batman is an unknown quantity in terms of his moral allegiances and the music emphasizes this quality: by writing for both Batman and Jack Napier in the whole-tone mode, and using unusual, synthesized percussion timbres for both of them, a sense of duality—a similarity in their moral positioning—is implied.

The use of the whole-tone mode in these two cues also establishes it as a signifier of 'dangerous spaces,' either physical or psychic, and how it is used in the rest of the film continues to play a part in how the differences and similarities between Batman and the Joker are represented musically. In "Roof Fight," the space is evidently physically dangerous: they are on a rooftop and, at one point, Batman hangs one of the muggers over the edge of the building. This in turn produces a psychological danger in terms of Batman's ability to be the hero of the piece: how far will he go? Is he simply a thug, no better than the criminals he is fighting? If he were to drop the mugger over the edge of the roof, then he would have crossed a line over which it would be morally very difficult to return, becoming a vengeful vigilante rather than upholder of the law.

In "Jack vs. Ekhart," the danger again operates on both physical and psychic levels. The physical danger becomes apparent as the tension between Jack and Eckhardt increases, climaxing musically and visually as Eckhardt pulls a gun on Jack, only to have Bob, Jack's trusty henchman, point a gun at him over Jack's shoulder. The space itself is not obviously dangerous in the way that the rooftop was, but the back alley is a transitional space, a borderland between the world of the law and that of the criminals, and the idea of transitional and, therefore, psychically unstable spaces is another aspect of the whole-tone scale's signification. It is similarly used in "Up Building," an extremely brief cue that effects the transition from outside to inside the criminal world, the camera shooting up the side of a skyscraper and into Grissom's penthouse office. This is a palpably dangerous space, the heart of the criminal operation.

Other aspects of "Jack vs. Ekhart" help, if not to establish Jack's musical representation, then to foreshadow the Joker's. The rhythm of the cue suggests a slightly warped tango. The tango is an urban dance originating from the late nineteenth-century Argentinean underworld, at which time it was often danced by two men (if only because they outnumbered women enormously in Buenos Aires at this time) and it has its own mythologies of knife fights and dueling. Given the barely suppressed hostility in this scene, the hints of tango in the rhythm of the cue add to the tension between the two main characters as well as hinting at Jack's catchphrase, heard much later in the film: "ever dance with the devil in the pale moonlight?" The idea of the Joker's connection with dancing and dance music, then, is one element he inherits from Jack.

The other important consideration in Jack-Joker's musical identity that is established here is the use of unusual timbres. The timbres in "Roof Fight" were slightly unusual, with a clearly nonorchestral, rising four-note motif, most noticeable at the start of the cue. Nonetheless, the orchestra plays most of that cue, while in "Jack vs. Ekhart" there is almost nothing in the conductor's score other than sparse string writing, a very low note reiterated by the piano, and a short section involving vibraphone and harp. Everything else is coming from Elfman's pre-laid synthesizer track, which utilizes a wide range of percussion sounds, complemented by the use of timbral effects from the orchestral instruments. The harp plays harmonics; the piano note is extremely low, giving it a rough texture that is exaggerated toward the end where it stutters rapidly and irregularly. The strings almost never play without a specified timbral coloring, such as *pizzicato*, *glissando*, or *sul tasto* (on the fingerboard, creating a very broad, mellow sound). At one point, the violins are marked *divisi* but again, the division is one of timbre rather than pitch: half are directed to play normally, while the other half play *sul ponticello* (on the bridge, creating a metallic sound). This attention to timbral detail in music for Jack-Joker is a key idea in how he is scored, in direct contrast to Bruce-Batman, who occupies a much more conventionally orchestral musical world. Jack's timbral irregularity is one of the first musical indicators that he is transgressing boundaries, existing sonically outside the normal confines of the Hollywood score that the main title cue established as Batman's territory.

In act 1, the cues are generally very clearly identified with either Jack or Bruce-Batman, for the simple reason that they are never in the same scene until the end of the act. However, Jack has no music that appears to be exclusively his. He shares the whole-tone scale with Batman and, although Jack's timbres are more extreme, Batman's "Roof Fight" cue also exploits unconventional timbral ideas. Batman, meanwhile, apparently has the Bat-theme as his musical property, with all the minor-key, tonal music that goes with it.

This position, however, becomes slightly more complicated in the cue following "Up Building," during the scene in Grissom's office. "Card Snap" begins at the point that Grissom puts Jack in charge of the Axis Chemicals job. This is an unusual cue in the score as a whole, as it is the only one to use an overtly jazz-influenced idiom. The most prominent instruments in the first part of the cue are vibraphone and saxophone, with a double bass (described in the score as a jazz solo bass) adding to the sense of a jazz ensemble embedded in the overall texture. The jazz-inflected scoring might plausibly be read as alluding to the well-established connection between jazz, crime dramas, and film noir, particularly given the visual coding of Grissom's men as 1930s' gangsters. However, this does not account for the fact that the composition also balances between the whole-tone mode and, curiously, the Bat-theme.

Although the first part of the cue is not in the whole-tone mode, there is a strong sense of whole-tone modalities in this section. At the same time, the saxophone hints at the opening notes of the Bat-theme as Alicia, seen from Jack's point of view, makes her entrance. This is immediately followed by an unequivocal statement of the Bat-theme by bassoon and lower strings as both Jack and Grissom watch her cross the room. Jack has previously asserted that Grissom does not know of their affair, but the series of glances between the characters strongly implies that he does, and it is at this point that the Bat-theme occurs. The use of what has thus far been firmly established as Batman's theme for one of Jack's scenes can be read in two different but complementary ways.

The first sees this as another aspect of Batman and Jack sharing music in this section of the film: the whole-tone mode and the Bat-theme are being used for both, apparently indiscriminately, blurring the musical distinctions between them. The use of the theme here even raises the possibility that Jack may be Batman, as at this point we have not met Bruce Wayne and, if an audience member were ignorant of the *Batman* continuity, it is conceivable that the theme's presence here, along with the use of whole-tone music in the earlier cues, might result in the inference that Jack is Batman. Whether this is inferred or not, their sharing of musical material strongly implies that Batman is operating outside the law: his music finds itself associated with the criminal element, just as the whole-tone scale, with its tonal ambiguities and association with the dangerous spaces and criminal activities of Gotham, is being used in cues associated with him.

The second reading makes a connection between Jack and the Joker's relationship with music and the fact that they have no music that is specifically and exclusively theirs. While the Joker compensates by appropriating music from a variety of sources, Jack lacks the hyper-self-awareness that the Joker appears to have of himself as a character in a narrative. In fact, whereas the Joker is larger than life and in glorious technicolor, Jack is very controlled and, notwithstanding his outright nastiness, arguably rather dull. His lack of a musical theme is one feature of his dullness, something that the Joker remedies with his self-conscious musical thievery—but it would appear that Jack is doing the same, albeit unwittingly. He nondiegetically appropriates the Bat-theme at a point in the film when the musical and, by implication, moral distinctions between Batman and the criminals are somewhat ill defined.

After the rest of the gang have left, the music underscoring the ensuing conversation between Grissom and Jack switches entirely into the whole-tone mode. Again, this is in keeping with the association this modality has with dangerous spaces and points of transition: what we are witnessing is Grissom reclaiming power within his own organization. Jack clearly does not want to go to Axis Chemicals but Grissom insists; and we know what Jack appears not to, that Grissom is aware of Jack's betrayal. The whole-tone mode alerts us to the danger within this encounter, a danger further confirmed when Grissom telephones Eckhardt after Jack departs, bringing the cue to an end.

The final two cues of act 1 clarify the musical positioning of Batman and Jack in support of the narrative's clarification of their moral positioning. "Axis Setup" is the third scene to score whole-tone modalities against Jack Napier and again marks a physically and psychically dangerous point in the narrative: he has broken into a space he should not be occupying and it will cause his downfall. This is as true of Jack's relationship with Alicia, which is Grissom's apparent motivation for the setup, as it is of his presence at Axis Chemicals—and the very name of the chemical works, Axis, further enforces the idea of transitions and unstable spaces, with this as a pivotal scene. In early drafts of the script, the factory was called Ace Chemicals, and the change of name indicates the importance of this scene in setting up the problems that the rest of the film must solve.[4]

At five-and-a-half minutes, "Shootout" is the longest cue in the score so far, written for the climactic scene of act 1.[5] The cue is built around an ostinato, a rolling minor-key figure heard in the lower strings that both lends a sense of pace to the action and creates a tension of its own (figure 5.1). As Charles Rosen has pointed out, an ostinato "is neither stable nor dynamic. . . . [It] creates instability . . . through the tension that comes through insistent repetition."[6] In the same way that insistence on the dominant creates a desire for resolution to the tonic, so insistence on a repeating figure creates the desire for resolution and change, and the longer it is denied, the greater the tension. Although this ostinato is clearly in 6/8, the cue is largely scored in 3/4, the technical reason for this being the number of cross-rhythms used against the ostinato, and the Bat-theme itself, which—on the relatively few occasions it is heard—is delivered firmly in 3/4.

Figure 5.1: "Shootout" Ostinato
Danny Elfman, Batman *Score, "Shootout," Bar 1*

This is the first time in the film that Batman and Jack have both been in a scene together, and this scene marks a turning point in both the narrative and in the way that music is used as part of the construction of their identities. Throughout the first part of the scene, as Jack attempts to escape and Gordon takes control of the situation from Eckhardt, the ostinato continues unabated (albeit with a few modulations) until Batman first appears, ambushing two members of Jack's gang. The Bat-theme makes its first appearance here, although only the first four notes are heard (figure 5.2a). Immediately afterward, it is restated in an altered form, the opening three notes replaced by a broken chord so that the first interval is now an ascending minor third (figure 5.2b). This interval links it directly to the ostinato's characteristic interval and to a descending minor-third motif that sounds in the horns at several points in the scene (figure 5.3). The underlying dominance of the Bat-theme's sound world—the minor key, the use of full orchestra—signal this as being Batman's territory, implying perhaps that this is a fight he will

Figure 5.2a: Four-Note Bat-Theme
Danny Elfman, Batman *Score, "Shootout," Bars 59–60*

Figure 5.2b: Broken-Chord Bat-Theme.
Danny Elfman, Batman *Score, "Shootout," Bars 64–66*

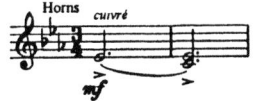

Figure 5.3: Falling Minor-Third Motif.
Danny Elfman, Batman *Score, "Shootout," Bars 10–11*

win. At the same time, the meter is, if slightly ambivalently, nonetheless moving in threes: the compound duple meter of the 6/8 ostinato does not diminish the sense that it is two groups of three, anticipating the Joker's appropriation of waltz-time as his meter. The territory is, therefore, ambivalent: Batman's by virtue of tonality, Jack's by virtue of meter—and the outcome of the scene supports this reading, as nobody can be said to win this particular battle.

As Batman leaves one of the gangsters swinging from a wire, the music returns to the basic ostinato pattern with question and answer motifs from brass and woodwind, but amid the cross-rhythms, the falling minor third motif reappears several times: first, as Commissioner Gordon catches his first glimpse of Batman standing on the catwalk above him; again as Jack looks anxiously for a way out; and then as the green chemicals that will soon be his downfall stream out of the vat he attacks with an axe. All is confusion: although all three of the forces of law, crime, and superheroism are seeking to be in control of the situation, the falling minor third, an inversion of the characteristic interval of both Bat-theme and ostinato, has an air of doom about it, of things that are not under control at all. As if to emphasize this, the cross-rhythms in the music increase against the regularity of the ostinato as both cops and crooks shoot all but blindly into the steam and fumes of the chemicals.

The Bat-theme reemerges briefly to identify Batman as we find him pursuing Jack along the mazelike catwalks, at which point the ostinato changes to a repeating-note figure in the upper strings, with the beats slightly unevenly accented (figure 5.4). The Bat-theme creeps back in again, initially with just its opening, rising whole-tone interval as Jack looks desperately around for an exit, and then in a more obviously recognizable form as Gordon ensures the exits are all blocked. However, as the theme implies, the person really preventing Napier's escape is Batman himself, the theme unequivocally representing Batman as a sonic as well as physical barrier to Jack's escape.

Figure 5.4: Strings Ostinato
Danny Elfman, Batman *Score, "Shootout," Bars 114–117*

As Jack realizes that he is in a position to shoot Gordon, the music shifts into the whole-tone mode, indicating that we have reached the axis point, the ultimately dangerous moment of the scene as a whole: things are coming to a head, and all three forces are about to come into direct and simultaneous conflict. Batman leaps in to save the Commissioner and his Bat-theme, in the minor broken-chord version heard earlier, accompanies him as he kicks the gun out of Napier's hand and grasps him by his collar, lifting him off the ground as he did the mugger in "Roof Fight." The minor broken-chord version of the Bat-theme should be announcing his moment of triumph but instantly, the music switches back to whole-tone modality. The rising string *tremolando* gives a ghostly whole-tone echo of the Bat-theme gesture preceding it, replacing Batman's expected triumph with a sudden transition into danger as Bob then raises his gun to the Commissioner's head (figure 5.5).

Figure 5.5: Whole-Tone Bat-Theme Echo.
Danny Elfman, Batman *Score, "Shootout," Bars 146–148*

The whole-tone music in this section is dominated by slow, rising whole-tone gestures, which in turn connect it back to the rising whole-tone interval of the Bat-theme, a motif we have just heard a few moments earlier. With this Bat-theme motif integrated into the whole-tone modality, we hear Batman's dilemma and the dangerous psychic space he finds himself in, torn between his personal desire to do away with Jack Napier and the moral imperative not to endanger the life of others, especially when the one being threatened in this case is the living symbol of the law. Batman's decision to let Jack go is both the best and worst decision he could make: it resolves the moral question about where he stands in relation to the law, which is reflected in the music after this cue, but it leads directly to the creation of the Joker.

After this scene, the whole-tone mode disappears from Batman's music: throughout act 2, it is a signifier solely of the Joker, his threats and his actions. Likewise, unorthodox timbres are specifically associated with the Joker's scoring and not Batman's after this point. The music, which throughout act 1 has served to create ideas of similarity between the two characters at numerous levels, reflects the outcome of the act: as Batman's moral positioning is clarified, so the division of musical materials reflects that clarification in act 2.

"Oppositional Duality" in the Music of Act 2

In act 1, ideas of duality between Batman and Jack are established largely by means of using the same musical material for both of them, and oppositional ideas are marginalized as the narrative encourages the viewer to regard Batman as morally ambivalent. Whether the narrative is successful in this or not is another question: Batman is too well-known a cultural icon for most of the audience to be fooled into thinking he is a possible villain rather than a hero, but there are clearly identifiable elements in both script and score that encourage a reading questioning Batman's heroic status. In act 2, those questions have been resolved: Batman is evidently an upholder of the law, and it would therefore seem more likely that ideas of opposition would be found in the music of this act. While this is indeed the case, ideas of duality remain, which is equally logical: the similarity between the two characters has now increased enormously. Where before there was only a potential similarity between them as two figures operating outside the structures of the law, now they are both 'freaks' created by extreme trauma, neither of them able to function normally in relation to the rest of the world. What is now created in the narrative and the music is an idea of oppositional duality, evident in the already described paralleling of their group of associates and in the inversion of their appearances, with Joker in multicolored clothing and 'whiteface' and Batman in practically monochrome Batsuit and black mask.[7]

Musically, the main indicator of the difference between Batman and the Joker is the use of the whole-tone scale. Within the nondiegetic underscore, the idea of oppositional duality resolves effectively into an association between tonal, minor-key scoring for Batman and use of the whole-tone scale for the Joker and the threat he poses. Hence we find the whole-tone scale being used in "Surgery," "Face Off," "Roasted Dude," in the "Photos" section of "Bruce Contemplates/Photos," in "Alicia's Mask," "Vicki Gets a Gift," and "Alicia's Unmasking." We find it being used for the Joker's men in "Street Fight," and as they pursue Batman and Vicki in the previous cue, "Batmobile Chase," where it alternates with Batman's minor-key tonal sections.

One other use of the whole-tone mode in act 2 makes this oppositional musical positioning even more explicit: when the Joker is in the ascendant, with his lethal cosmetics terrorizing Gotham, a *Citizen Kane*–style spinning newspaper headline of "Cosmetics Scare In Gotham. Product Tampering Claims Thirteen Lives. Who Is This Mysterious "Joker"?" is accompanied by the cue "Paper Spin," written in whole-tone mode to indicate the Joker's dominance at this point. When Batman foils his plan, we have a second newspaper headline, this time seen as a deliveryman throws a bundle of newspapers onto the pavement by a news kiosk: "Batman Cracks Joker's Poison Code!" In contrast to the previous scene, the cue "Paper Throw" claims Batman's victory: the music is firmly in a minor key and the Bat-theme is heard in the horns as we see the headline.

The Joker: Music, Appropriation and Self-Consciousness

Jack Napier has, to all intents and purposes, ceased to exist by the beginning of act 2, to be replaced by the Joker. One of the principal differences between Jack and the Joker is their relationship with music. Jack has no special relationship with music at all: our first sight of him in act 1 is musically silent, and he has no musical theme to compete with Batman's, although he does have an association with unusual timbres. In act 2, the Joker retains this timbral idea and lays claim to the whole-tone scale but, in addition to this, he has a unique relationship with music that frequently elides diegetic and nondiegetic scoring.

The Joker's first scene and cue is "Surgery," although we do not see his postaccident face. Everything here is in a state of flux: we do not know what has happened to Jack after his fall into the chemicals, and this uncertainty is mirrored in the music, in what is probably the most discordant cue in the score. It combines whole-tone composition with entirely atonal passages, moving in and out of whole-tone tonality, sometimes using it on its own, sometimes with atonal additions and sometimes abandoning it altogether. The music is highly fragmented and disjointed, the apparent lack of thematic connection between the gestures sounding quite chaotic. The cue never settles, never establishes a coherent musical identity, and this corresponds to the idea that the character is no longer Jack Napier, but we do not know who or what he has become. The transitional nature of the scene is indicated by the presence of the whole-tone mode, but the cue also keeps suggesting that it is about to launch into a new theme, which it never does. The rising atonal phrase as the doctor starts to unwind the bandages is one of these false leads, as is the sustained high violin note as Jack-Joker looks at himself in the mirror. No melody emerges, however, and the music reverts to its chaotic gestures.

As a whole, the cue reestablishes the connection between Jack-Joker and the use of timbre as a key element. The strings, again, use an assortment of timbral colorings including *tremolandi, glissandi,* using mutes, playing *sul tasto, a punta d'arco* (on the tip of the bow), and playing harmonics, and with another timbral *divisi* section, where half the violins play with vibrato and the other half without. The cue climaxes with a passage of extreme trilling that creates a dense, tense texture (figure 5.6).

Figure 5.6: Strings Trilling Passage
Danny Elfman, Batman *Score, "Surgery," Bar 29*

In the next cue for the Joker, the questions surrounding his new identity and new musical identity are simultaneously resolved. "Face Off" underscores the scene in which the Joker reveals himself and takes revenge on Grissom. The first part of the cue completes the process of transition from Jack to Joker, confirming his association with the whole-tone scale while preserving the association of the whole-tone mode with the ideas of boundaries, dangerous spaces, and transitional points. "Jack" stands in shadow, the whole-tone music accompanying his confrontation with Grissom. At the end of the whole-tone section, he crosses the boundary created by the light, stepping out of the shadow to reveal his new face for the first time and naming himself "Joker."

The music in the first section of this cue is as fragmented and unsettled as it was in "Surgery," with great use of *glissandi, tremolandi,* and trills in the strings and in the percussion, although the texture is far less disjointed than before. When the Joker reveals himself to Grissom and to us, allowing us to see him in his bizarrely colored, whitefaced glory, the music stops quite abruptly and then returns, as utterly transformed as he himself is. He proceeds to murder Grissom to the accompaniment of the Straussian waltz arranged for full orchestra: the combination of the Joker's appearance, his antics, and the music combine to create a sense of circus, albeit a grotesque and dangerous one, the more dangerous for having turned a murder into an ungraceful, comic dance set to an otherwise elegant waltz. Although the waltz is in a major key, it climaxes in the minor as the Joker discovers his gun is empty, shrugs, and then raises his arms in triumph as if acknowledging the applause of an unseen audience.

This is the first clear instance of the Joker appropriating music for himself, and the first time we witness his apparent awareness of his musical environment. His behavior, the way he prances and twists as he shoots Grissom, makes much less sense if we suppose him to be oblivious of the underscore. Jack Napier was clearly not aware of the underscore in the previous scene in Grissom's apartment, but his transformation into the Joker has given him a new relationship with the diegesis of the film he inhabits. This can be read as metadiegesis, of the audience being able to hear the music that the Joker is hearing in his own mind's ear. However, it is a little more complicated than straightforward metadiegesis, as there is a self-consciousness in the way that the Joker is hearing this music that suggests that he has effectively taken control of the film's soundtrack and is using it to his own ends: he is writing his own underscore, selecting pieces of music in the same way a music editor might to create a temp track. Danny Elfman, it would seem, has not provided the Joker with a theme, so he has appropriated a body of music for himself, a reading that automatically attributes to him an awareness that he exists within the narrative construct of a film. Again, as his timbral idiosyncrasies mark him as transgressive in comparison to the acceptable timbres of Batman's classical Hollywood orchestra, so his self-conscious relationship with the film's nondiegetic underscore marks him as transgressive in comparison to the way that Batman and all the other characters are contained by the film's diegesis. He is not contained: although he never turns to camera and addresses the audience directly in the way that, for example, Rob Gordon (John Cusack) does in *High Fidelity* (Stephen Frears, 2000), nonetheless, his awareness of the music issuing from the underscore places him in a position of power over his environment that Batman does not share.

The Joker's use of music becomes unambiguously diegetic in sub-sequent scenes and equally overtly connected with his violence. In his first meeting with the gang bosses, he sings "There'll be a hot one in the old town tonight" as he murders Anton. When he goes to the museum to meet Vicki, he accompanies his actions with music on a portable cas-sette player, with Prince's "Partyman" for the sequence where he and his gang 'improve the paintings,' and then an easy-listening arrange-ment of Max Steiner's theme from *A Summer Place* to underscore his conversation with an understandably frightened Vicki. None of these exist as cues in Elfman's scores but there is one entirely diegetic cue that does, namely "Joker's Commercial," the accompaniment to the Joker's announcement of his lethal cosmetics. The cue is in a similar idiom to *A Summer Place,* pastiche easy-listening, but now brightly up-tempo. The music itself is jaunty and fun: this is a prime example of Elfman's 'quirky' music, where the brightness of the composition contrasts with and serves to exaggerate the grotesque nature of the Joker's revelations about his products. The orchestration of "Joker's Commercial" is very much in keeping with both the light music idiom and the Joker's usual palette of colors—*pizzicato* strings, glockenspiel, and vibraphone—but with the melody taken by woodwind and by brass, the brass timbres varied with different mutes. A particular feature of the cue is a musical 'shrug' gesture where the melody rises to a high point and then comes to a brief stop before restarting again lower down (figure 5.7a). This same gesture is also found in the Straussian waltz (figure 5.7b) and, in both cases, it contributes to the sense of carefree, almost blasé joy that the Joker experiences in these scenes, a devil-may-care attitude to his own violent antics.

Figure 5.7a: Joker's Shrug Gesture
Danny Elfman, Batman *Score, "Joker's Commercial," Bars 3–4*

Figure 5.7b: Joker's Shrug Gesture
Danny Elfman, Batman *Score, "Face Off," Bars 47–50*

The Joker's appropriations are not entirely restricted to popular music and waltzes. There are two points in the score of act 2 where, as in "Card Snap," the Bat-theme is heard apparently accompanying the Joker. The first occasion is at the end of "Beddy Bye," at the end of the series of scenes alternating between the start of Bruce and Vicki's affair and the birth of the Joker that begins act 2. A short sequence of brass chords segues from the bedroom to the Joker in Grissom's office, where the celeste plays a speeded-up version of his Straussian waltz, accompanied by a few brief, interestingly atonal gestures from timpani and bassoon. The music is simultaneously playful, sweet, and disconcerting. The music-box chimes of the celeste create a musical image that contradicts the violent murder we have just witnessed. As the Joker reads the blood-spattered headline "Winged Freak Terrorizes Gotham," the celeste tune changes to a speeded-up, 6/8 version of the Bat-theme, continuing as the Joker does an impression of what a 'winged freak' might sound like, although his "whoop whoop" sounds more like an owl than bat. Nonetheless, musically this brings back together the two strands of the narrative that have been separated by the alternating-scene sequence. The Joker's words and Batman's theme in the underscore make it clear that a confrontation between these two is unavoidable and essential. Although Batman is not physically present in the scene, the newspaper headline indicates his presence in the Joker's thoughts, and the music underlines this. There is no sense here that the Bat-theme is referring to anyone other than Batman.

The second use of the Bat-theme in association with the Joker occurs in "Clown Attack," the scene where the Joker makes his first public appearance, murdering the gang boss who is attempting to take over Grissom's empire. A slightly augmented, waltzing version of the Bat-theme plays as he turns triumphantly to face the world, his arms spread wide, and his unavoidable smile even wider than usual (figure 5.8). The fact that its arrangement here echoes his own Strauss waltz underlines the fact that that we are hearing a juxtaposition of the Joker's waltz meter with Batman's theme. As mentioned in chapter 2, Elfman composes chronologically once he has his basic thematic material established and during this almost stream-of-consciousness process, sometimes the 'wrong' theme will find itself being used, as in the use of Ichabod's music over scenes that are entirely about the Headless Horseman. This appearance of the Bat-theme in the wrong place in fact works very effectively: Bruce-Batman is present in this scene, which is part of the sequence in which Vicki follows and observes Bruce. There are multi-

Figure 5.8: Waltz Version of the Bat-Theme
Danny Elfman, Batman *Score, "Clown Attack," Bars 47–50*

ple points of view in the scene: we are watching Vicki watching Bruce watching the Joker, and in the first part of the scene, the ambivalence of the point of view from which we are seeing events is not helped by the music. The cue uses thematic ideas from the Bat-theme, but combines these with timbres and gestures associated with the Joker. The first point in the cue that a full statement of the Bat-theme is heard is when it appears as a waltz for the triumphant Joker, and the visual gesture as he turns, as if to acknowledge the applause of his audience immediately after having committed a murder, mirrors the same gesture at the end of the "Face Off" waltz when he discovered his gun was empty after killing Grissom. The subversion of the Bat-theme to the same waltzing rhythm that marked the earlier murder reflects the Joker's triumph and his success at this point in the ruthless pursuit of power that propels him through the narrative. At the same time, it is also the point at which Bruce recognizes the Joker as the former Jack Napier. The Joker has already decided that Batman is a threat that must be overcome, but this is the moment when Bruce comes to his own realization that Jack was not killed at Axis Chemicals and that Batman still has a battle ahead of him. The appearance of the theme at this point has a dual nature—the waltz connects it to the Joker, the melody to Batman—but the way that the Joker appears to appropriate the theme acts as a kind of musical challenge, a threat to Batman's ownership of the theme that signifies a threat to his power, and the appearance of the theme in the form it is given here becomes a symbol of the Joker's attempts to wrest power away from Batman in the final act.

A Pair of Love Themes

While the Joker's relationship with musical diegesis is one of the main ways in which straightforward ideas of difference between him and Bruce-Batman are created, one of the clearest examples of their op-positional duality is the presence of parallel love themes for Vicki, one from Bruce's point of view and one from the Joker's. Bruce's love theme is derived from the accompaniment motif in "Scandalous," and there is convincing musical evidence that this is Bruce Wayne's theme rather than Vicki's. Batman's theme is a five-note theme in a minor key: it starts with a stepwise rise to the minor third, which then leaps up to the minor sixth, and finally falls back to the fifth (figure 5.9a). The Love theme is identical with two small but important exceptions: first, it is in a major key; second, it does not begin on the tonic but on the mediant, and as a result the first interval rises by a minor second instead of a major second (figure 5.9b). The Bat-theme and the Love theme, therefore, can be seen as two sides of a musical coin, a thematic metaphor for the duality of Batman and Bruce Wayne encoded in the brooding minor-key theme and its major key, romantic doppelgänger. The Love theme is clearly designed to act as Elfman's typical secondary theme, one that is often similar to the principal theme but generally much less used and assigned to more reflective moments within Elfman's action scores as discussed in chapter 2.

Figure 5.9a: Melodic Outline of Elfman's Bat-Theme

Figure 5.9b: Melodic Outline of the Love Theme
Danny Elfman, Batman Score, "Kitchen Dinner," Bars 20–21

Using a theme derived from the accompaniment of a Prince song for Bruce Wayne's character might, on the one hand, appear to undermine the position of Prince's songs as part of the Joker's musical identity, particularly given that if any side of Bruce-Batman duality was going to be aligned with the Joker, one would imagine it would be Batman, not Bruce. However, the fact that the theme does not appear in the film within the context of the song prevents it from being identified with Prince until the narrative is completed, so preserving the foregrounded Prince numbers in the score as the Joker's territory.

Bruce's Love theme is the first music heard in act 2. Its orchestration is quite different from that of the main Bat-theme, using flute, oboe, electric piano, strings, and harp, while the texture is also quite different. Gone is the theme-driven, busy music of Batman's cues, with their distinctive rapid countermotives from strings and high woodwind against melodies in low woodwind and brass. Instead, the textures are soft and drifting, almost impressionistic.

The Love theme does not emerge immediately: Vicki and Bruce are having dinner at opposite ends of an absurdly long table in a cavernous dining room. The dining room scene itself has no underscore, the echoing silence of the vast room and extreme length of the table being used to make the scene seem cold and uncomfortable, a feature of several of the couple's other scenes together created by the omission of the cues written for them. A single statement of the Love theme is heard as they leave this room, and the hesitance with which it emerges to warm the silence of their encounter reflects the hesitance of Bruce himself, his inarticulateness and gaucheness in this unaccustomed social situation.

After they have moved to the kitchen to complete their dinner in less formal surroundings, Bruce and Vicki talk about their families and childhoods. Strings, woodwind, and electric piano play gently rocking major-key chords, but there is no clear melodic theme as such. Again, there is a hesitancy, a reluctance in the music to state its theme clearly that reflects Bruce's own shyness and reluctance to become emotionally entangled. The first hint of melody comes in with the harp arpeggios and a descending broken-chord motif from the oboe, but the music, for the most part, appears to be working very hard at not drawing attention to itself. Its soft, stable, tonal, and quite homogenous texture is very different from anything else heard in the score so far. Right at the end of the cue and the scene, the Love theme is finally heard, again stated only once in unison by violin, harp, oboe, and horn, the only time a brass instrument is heard in this cue.[8]

In direct contrast, the Joker, on his first sighting of Vicki in a photograph taken by Bob, instantly acquires his own rival love theme, "Beautiful Dreamer." There is no hesitation, no reluctance on his part to stake an emotional claim to Vicki. His theme also has very distinctive orchestration in similar registers to Bruce's but, as might be expected, it uses rather more unorthodox timbres. The Joker's theme also uses harp and strings, but includes celeste and vibraphone instead of the woodwind and piano of Bruce's theme, and the effect is a parody of romance. Bruce's theme is very understated, orchestrated to create a gently moving, quite sparse texture that describes Bruce's shyness. The Joker's version is full of 'shimmer': the acoustic effect of the celeste, vibraphone, and violins is of an overproduced, overreverberant texture, the excessive smoothness of the strings seeming contrived in comparison to the simplicity of Bruce's theme.

For a variety of reasons, the Joker's love theme does not seem sincere, precisely because it taps into a well-established code for cinematic romance. The use of an established standard song as a signifier of love is a convention of romantic films, particularly romantic comedies. It can be seen in the existence of 'title song' films such as *Pretty Woman* (1990) and *Only You* (1994), where the song and its lyric are central to the narrative and its music. It is similarly seen in the usually nondiegetic presence of standard songs within romantic comedy in general, which has resulted in them becoming one of "the 'heavily conventional' signs of old-fashioned romance that make credible the films' preoccupation with a belief in 'true love'."[9] The fact that the songs generally occur nondiegetically, and frequently either in main title or montage sequences, is part of what allows them to function as a signifier of love: they rarely have to compete with dialogue and so there is a focus on the lyrics, which become an aspect of how the narrative is conveyed and how the theme of romantic love is privileged within it. The central couple are rarely conscious of the song: it tends to represent their true but unspoken emotions, allowing us to believe that they are in love even if they are hiding this fact from each other throughout most of the film.

The Joker, however, subverts this code, using a standard song, but removing its lyrics and using it self-consciously rather than as an element of the nondiegetic underscore. The removal of the lyrics is important, as is the fact that the song underscores dialogue rather than being allowed to stand alone. The fact that we know Vicki is already in love with the hero of the film also makes it unlikely that we will hear this music as a signifier of true love, and if it cannot signify true love, it cannot be read as sincere.

Additionally, the Joker's attraction to Vicki's photographic image is set against this music on the one hand, and against other photographic images of grinning corpses on the other, which the Joker is cutting out for his own amusement, a perverse scrapbook collection. We have also already heard the Joker's other waltz appropriation, the Strauss pastiche, used as a grotesque accompaniment to murder: the Joker's ability to make these musical appropriations was established in connection to his violent behavior. Because of this, "Beautiful Dreamer," another elegant waltz, acquires a grotesque veneer rather than a romantic one, and the result is that the music appears to present the Joker's attachment to Vicki as not simply insincere but as a potentially very dangerous parody of romance.

The Joker's self-conscious relationship with music also means that it appears to be he himself who is doing the musical parodying. Bruce's Love theme arises from his Batman music: it is part of him, an expression of his own identity, but one that occurs in the nondiegetic scoring. He is, however, entirely unconscious of it, which makes it emotionally much more convincing, in the same way that the nondiegetic use of songs in romantic comedy enhances the impression of their credibility as expressions of love. Bruce is not trying to produce a love theme: it is happening quite naturally, in terms of our acceptance of the 'naturalness' of film conventions regarding music. The theme communicates his point of view, giving us an insight into his emotional response to Vicki. By contrast, the Joker's theme is not actually his: it is an easily recognizable appropriation of a piece of popular music, and the way it is used in the film makes it seem that he is using it consciously and intentionally: this is how he is hearing and sonically describing his attraction to Vicki. It is arch, it is camp, and it is not romantically charged in the way that Bruce's spontaneous and unconscious musical response appears to be. Moreover, in the final confrontation at the end of the film, the Joker refers to himself and Vicki as Beauty and the Beast, but then makes it clear that he is Beauty. This in turn suggests that the "Beautiful Dreamer" of the song is himself rather than Vicki, adding to the sense of parody.

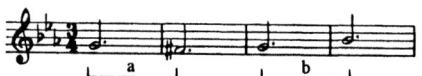

Figure 5.10a: Waltz Theme
Danny Elfman, Batman *Score, "Waltz," Bars 73–76*

Figure 5.10b: Inverted Motifs from the Waltz Theme
Danny Elfman, Batman *Score, "Photos," Bars 20–23*

We hear the Joker's love theme as he sees Vicki's photograph: it bursts abruptly out of the underscore, halting the existing music in its tracks as he utters the words "stop the press." Until this point, the underscore has been typically Jokeresque: the music is in a waltz rhythm and the melody, played by the timbrally idiosyncratic combination of musical saw and saxophone, is a variation and inversion of the Strauss waltz (figures 5.10a and b). As he sets eyes on Vicki, the music instantly changes, as if her image summons the music in his mind's ear, an impression strengthened when he begins to dance, twirling around to the "Beautiful Dreamer" waltz, still holding Vicki's picture. Later, in Vicki's apartment, we hear "Beautiful Dreamer" again, but now it is being played diegetically on a portable cassette player. The Joker's ability to lift the music out of the underscore and into the narrative confirms the music's earlier metadiegetic status, and further demonstrates the Joker's power over his musical environment.

Vicki

Neither of the two love themes really tells us anything about Vicki. In both cases, the themes tell us far more about the character whose point of view they represent than they do about the object of their passion. In the same way that the Bat-theme describes Batman, so Bruce's Love theme, being derived from it, describes Bruce—gentle, and reluctant to state itself clearly. Likewise, there is nothing of Vicki in "Beautiful Dreamer," only the glibly saccharine distortion of romance that the Joker wishes to impose upon her. Although flutes and oboes often characterize the music heard when she is on-screen, they tend to represent her presence rather than her point of view. Vicki, the third principal character of this film, generally remains the object of the other principals' music, rarely acquiring a musical subjectivity of her own.

There are, nonetheless, a small number of occasions when the music can be interpreted as representing Vicki's point of view, one of these being "Batcave." This cue occurs in the Batcave after Batman has rescued her from the museum, during the scene in which he tells her how the Joker's poison works and gives her a dossier to take to the press. The music of this cue is primarily in 3/4, the Joker's waltz meter, and is using his orchestration—vibraphone, harps playing harmonics, *tremolando* strings, open string harmonic *glissandi*, and muted trumpet—along with Vicki's flute and oboe. As Vicki first sees the bats hanging from the walls of the cave, the flute plays a minor-key version of the Joker's waltz. Although this is in a minor key, which is the Bat-theme's tonality, there is no sharpened seventh in the melody, with the result that the melody hints at the Joker's whole-tone mode. Although this is a scene entirely between Batman and Vicki, the Bat-theme is missing until the final few bars. The Joker-coded music is present right from the start, although the accompanying arpeggios are arguably a version of the Bat-theme, reminiscent of the broken-chord version heard in "Shootout." The only statement of the Bat-theme in "Batcave" is a broken-chord version right at the end of the cue, as Batman appears to attack Vicki with a vampirelike sweep of his cape (figure 5.11). However, apart from this, the Bat-theme is notable for its absence from the underscore, the only time in the film that Batman's visual image and theme are decoupled so comprehensively. As with the earlier use of the Bat-theme for Jack Napier, this use of what appears to be the Joker's music for Batman can be read in more than one way.

Most of this scene is ostensibly about the Joker: Batman has brought Vicki to the cave to tell her what he has discovered about the Joker's poisoned products, and this in itself could account for why the Joker's music is so prevalent in this scene. However, this is the scene where Vicki tells Batman "a lot of people think you're as dangerous as the Joker" and "you're not exactly normal, are you?" This cue is part of a chronologically unbroken sequence that begins with Vicki thinking she is going on a date with Bruce, instead meeting the Joker in an environment of his choosing and now finding herself alone with Batman in an environment he has chosen. For the preceding twelve minutes of the film, Vicki has been threatened, terrified, attacked with acid, dramatically snatched from the museum by a masked man in an all-encasing black rubber bodysuit, been driven at high speed through Gotham, nearly crashing more than once, and has been chased on foot by gun and sword-wielding thugs. She has reverse-abseiled up a building, been insulted about her weight, watched Batman nearly get run over by his own car, and then been driven out into the middle of nowhere and through an apparently solid rock wall. She has then found herself in a cave full of bats and has almost fallen from the top of the Batmobile's platform into a chasm. All in all, it has not been a good evening for Vicki, and the music here is effectively her point of view—she does not know if Batman is any less dangerous than the Joker was and so she 'hears' him as the Joker, his orchestration, his appropriated theme, albeit it not one of the ones he played to her in the museum. Her own voice is present in the flute and oboe melodic line, like a musical question mark as to whether she can trust Batman. The music communicates her unease in this unsettled and chromatic cue that shifts between major and minor modalities; and it also indicates the extent to which he is currently not clearly differentiated from the Joker in her eyes. The use of the Bat-theme at the end does little to resolve this. It states a version of his theme but it remains in the Joker's 3/4 meter and reverses the normal polarities of the theme, being given in a major-key version that, with its switch from major third to minor sixth, sounds more chromatic and more threatening than it does in its usual minor key (see figure 5.11). In addition, the theme does not resolve to its fifth note, leaving Vicki's questions unanswered: he is no less of a threat at the end of the scene than he was at the start, and his line of dialogue at the point the theme is heard reinforces this as he says "there is something else you have that I want" before enveloping her in his cape, à la Dracula. There is a clear suggestion that Batman may be about to take advantage of the vulnerable Vicki, an impression that is encouraged as the end of the cue segues to Vicki's apartment the following morning. We find Vicki lying face down on her bed, her dress somewhat askew, and only after she regains consciousness do we discover that the thing he wanted was the film and the pictures of him she shot the night before.

Figure 5.11: Major Arpeggio Bat-Theme
Danny Elfman, Batman *Score, "Batcave," Bar 59*

Act 3: The Final Conflict

The function of act 3 is to resolve the conflict initiated in act 1. In many respects, Batman suffers from the same problem as Hamlet: throughout act 2, he fails to act effectively against the Joker, even though he knows him to be a murderer. There was a clear opportunity to challenge him at the museum, which would probably not have endangered Vicki anymore than the action Batman did take; and it is hard to understand what Batman hoped to achieve with his behavior in Vicki's apartment when he attempted to goad the Joker to 'get nuts.' The fact that he had placed a silver tray in his jacket—which then stopped the bullet the Joker fired at him—implies that he expected to be attacked, but he could not have predicted that the Joker would then simply leave Vicki alone and unharmed, so his failure to take effective action to defeat the Joker has endangered her and everyone else in Gotham.

Like Hamlet, Batman needs a final push to make him take direct action. In the apartment scene, just before he shoots Bruce, the Joker asks the question: "ever dance with the devil in the pale moonlight?" This phrase triggers Bruce's memory of his parents' murder and near

the end of act 2, during the cue "Challenge/Dream," we see Bruce realize that it was the young Jack Napier who killed his parents and caused
the trauma that led to the creation of Batman. This gives him a reason
for pursuing the Joker, but the reason leads to the strong possibility that
Batman is now purely motivated by the need for personal revenge. This
in turn repositions him as a potentially vengeful vigilante rather than a
just warrior, acting to serve his own ends rather than greater good. The
music of act 3, therefore, returns to some of the ideas used in act 1 that
created a sense of duality—of moral similarity—between Batman and
the Joker. The music itself also acts as one of the sites of conflict as
protagonist and antagonist battle for dominance.

The most obvious way in which the idea of Batman's moral ambivalence is reestablished is through the use of the whole-tone scale. In act
1, the whole-tone scale was used for both Batman and Jack, and had a
clear association with the idea of dangerous and transitional spaces. In
act 2, it retained this association with danger, but became the musical
preserve of the Joker. However, in act 3, it once again becomes associated with Batman and his actions.

The whole-tone scale is heard intermittently throughout "Batwing
IIA," the main cue underscoring the conflict between Batman and the
Joker at the festival parade. In the same way that minor-key Bat-theme
sections and whole-tone sections alternated in the earlier "Batmobile
Chase," so they alternate again here. "Batwing IIA" makes great use
of a rising whole-tone motif that, as the first interval of the Bat-theme,
has an obvious connection to Batman. However, it is used here primarily in connection with the Joker's actions, while later parts of the cue
switch from the Bat-theme's minor-key tonality to the Joker's whole-
tone mode. The insistence on the major second interval in "Batwing
IIA" is, therefore, simultaneously a Bat-theme signifier but one that is
threatened by the Joker in that it anticipates the whole-tone mode. The
music could 'switch sides' at any moment, prepared by the rising major
second, which has the potential to act as a pivot between the two tonalities as seen in the previous major conflict between these two characters
in "Shootout."

In the sequence of cues from "Rescue" to "Street Fight," the whole-
tone sections were all explicitly associated with the Joker, his henchmen, and the threat that they pose to the escaping Batman and Vicki: the
one extended section of whole-tone music that scores the couple rather
than the henchmen in this section is the sequence when they are forced
to abandon the safety of the Batmobile, running through the streets to

escape their pursuers. The whole-tone music represents those pursuers and the dangerous space that Bruce and Vicki have been forced into by them, and so can still be read as an aspect of the Joker's musical representation rather than Batman's. In "Batwing IIA," there are two specific occasions when the use of the whole-tone scale and the Bat-theme muddies the previously clear moral ground between them. First, the Bat-theme is used for what is potentially the Joker's moment of triumph, as his balloons fill up with and start to disperse their poisonous gas; then the whole-tone scale is used for Batman's countering action. Having captured the balloons, the whole-tone mode is used for the music as he narrowly misses crashing into a building and successfully escapes to take the balloons up and away from Gotham's streets. This is the first time since act 1 that the Bat-theme has unambiguously been used for an action of the Joker's and the first time since act 1 that the whole-tone mode has been used so specifically for Batman's actions. It retains its former meanings: Batman is in a literally tight spot, a dangerous physical space that he must negotiate in order to escape from the labyrinth of Gotham's streets into the night sky. Nonetheless, we have not heard this mode being used in this way for him since "Shootout."

If Batman's moral ambiguity is hinted at in this brief moment, it is made explicit at the end of "Showdown A," which underscores the confrontation in the belfry. The Joker is unarmed, Batman has disposed of all his henchmen, and the just warrior should now, by rights, take the villain into custody and hand him over to the police. Instead, Batman appears to kill the Joker in cold blood. He relentlessly advances upon his adversary, attacks him, and eventually punches him so hard that the Joker falls backward over the parapet of the cathedral tower, apparently to his death. Most of the cue is tonal, but this final event, as Batman crosses the line between just warrior and vigilante, is scored with a brief flourish in the whole-tone mode. In terms of the way that whole-tone music has been used throughout the film, this scoring means that his actions cannot be read as heroic or just: he has crossed the boundary into the Joker's moral territory.

It is, fortunately, a lapse from which Batman can be rescued, as the Joker is not killed. As Batman and Vicki peer over the edge of the balustrade, the Joker grabs them and pulls them over, reversing their physical positions and at the same time, reversing the identification of music and character back to their normal symbolic positions, with the Joker associated with the whole-tone mode as he taunts and threatens Vicki and Batman. When he finally falls to his death down the side of the cathedral tower, the whole-tone writing for this affirms the undoubted danger of this transitional space, just as it does again when moments later Batman and Vicki also fall. Rather than becoming the Joker's post-mortem victims, they are saved by one of Batman's gadgets, and the music returns to the safety of Bruce-Batman's tonality at that point.

Despite the moments of ambiguity, ideas of opposition between Batman and the Joker persist in act 3 in ways quite close to those of act 2, with tonal music and the Bat-theme largely being used for Batman's actions and the whole-tone and other musics being used for the Joker. The diegetic and metadiegetic aspects of the Joker's use of music also persist. Prince's "Trust" features diegetically in the festival parade as the Joker rides on his birthday-cake float, while the Straussian waltz reappears metadiegetically in the cue "Waltz," for the battle between Batman and the Joker's henchman as the Joker waltzes with a semi-conscious Vicki in the background. This, and his comment, "shall we dance?" to Batman just before the cue starts again positions this as music that the Joker has control over: it is more than simply heard in his head. The editing of the fight going on between Batman and the henchmen seems choreographed: metaphorically and literally, Batman, like Vicki, is dancing to the Joker's tune.

The Strauss waltz was the first piece of music to which the Joker laid claim, and the musical appropriation in "Face Off" marked his appropriation of power from Grissom, whom he condemned for having set Jack up "over a woman," Alicia. This second waltz marks the point when he finally loses his power to Batman and once again, a woman, Vicki, is the apparent field of dispute, although in both cases the woman is somewhat incidental: what is really at stake is power. The two waltzes frame the Joker's career, and if the first marked his ascent, then the second must bring him down.

The waltz appears here as a rondo, taking the form AABACADACA, where the A section is the waltz theme as heard in "Face Off." This is obviously a far more extended version of the waltz than previously heard and during the cue there are moments when the music itself becomes a site of conflict. The A section is major key but several of the episodes are in the minor key and each time these slips to the minor occur, the music moves toward the territory of the Bat-theme, particularly in the broken-chord accompaniment figures that so closely resemble some of its versions, and in the chromatic falling melody of the C section (figure 5.12), which echoes the way the end of the Bat-theme characteristically falls from the minor sixth to the fifth and then to the augmented fourth, both features that can be seen in figure 5.2b. The D section, which is the climax of the fight where the final henchman is eventually toppled down the stairwell of the tower, introduces a variant of the Bat-theme that competes with the waltz melody itself. This appears at the moment that the henchman appears to throw Batman down the stairwell, only to have the tables turned and to fall himself—very similar to the reversal a few minutes later when Batman throws the Joker over the balustrade.

Figure 5.12: Chromatic Falling Melody
Danny Elfman, Batman *Score, "Waltz," Bars 89–96*

Again, this can be read in two ways. The use of the Bat-theme within the Joker's waltz might be read as another attempt by the Joker to appropriate the Bat-theme, absorbing it into his own music in a manner not dissimilar to the way he seems to conjure the Bat-theme out of the nondiegetic underscore in "Clown Attack" and earlier in act 3. However, the Joker is barely present in this cue: he is visible occasionally in the background, waltzing with Vicki on the balcony and apparently oblivious to the fight that is going on in the belfry. The focus of our attention is Batman himself, and the appearance of the Bat-theme within the waltz might also be read as the first and only time that Batman appropriates and manipulates the Joker's music to his own. If the Joker's metadiegetic use of music is an indicator of the way in which he transgresses the diegesis of the narrative, then we can interpret the Bat-theme endeavoring to impose itself on the waltz as Batman attempting to clip the Joker's wings, constraining and recontaining him and his music and forcing them to submit to the diegesis of the film and score.

Overall, one of the most distinctive features of the musical representation of the Joker is the fragmentary and diverse nature of the music associated with him, with the use of unusual timbres and of four quite different genres: the Strauss waltz, "Beautiful Dreamer" and the easy-listening idiom, the whole-tone music, and the Prince songs. This diversity is itself an indication of the instability and irrationality of the Joker's character—it refuses to cohere, instead accumulating multiple identifications. The Joker, as his name indicates, is a wild card, unpredictable, and therefore difficult to pin down or contain. In the end, the only way to contain him is to kill him, but even in death he resists and reasserts his musical irrationality: the final section of his scoring, at the end of "Showdown II" combines all the distinctive elements of his music utilized in Elfman's score: the theme of the Strauss waltz played by celeste, "Beautiful Dreamer" on glockenspiel played with knitting needles, and insistent tritones from flutes and vibraphone, a reference to the whole-tone scale.

Batman, meanwhile, is entirely rehabilitated from his momentary moral lapse by the fact that he is ultimately absolved of responsibility for the Joker's death. Not only is the Joker's last line "sometimes I just kill myself," but had he given up his escape attempt after Batman's Bat-bolo tied him to the gargoyle, he would probably have survived, albeit hanging upside down from the top of a cathedral, just as Vicki and Batman survive, hanging the right way up halfway down the cathedral. With this victory, all ambiguity disappears from Batman's scoring and the final two cues of the film, the "Finale" and "End Credits" triumphantly restate the heroic Bat-theme.

Chapter 6

Reading the Score:
Part II

The Bat-Theme

Unlike the Joker, whose musical fragmentation positions him as ultimately incoherent and irrational, Batman's theme serves to create the opposite positioning, of a figure who is established by the end of the film as both coherent and authoritative. Batman actively seems to want to be contained by and integrated into the diegetic reality of his universe, while the Joker is an enthusiastic crosser of boundaries. The Joker's trajectory through the film is characterized by transgression, action, and a destructive pursuit of power. Batman's, meanwhile, is characterized by a desire to be socially and romantically 'normal,' by reaction rather than by action—particularly after the opening scene—and by a desire to find a morally acceptable place within the social structure. This is, however, not an easy process, and is marked by moments of ambivalence, setbacks, and outright failures before Batman's ultimate social, romantic, and heroic triumph.

As has been previously argued, the one true theme in the *Batman* score is the five-note Bat-theme itself. The whole-tone music is not thematic in the same way, as it has no melody or specific motif that serves as a theme: rather, the idiom of the whole-tone scale serves as a signifier in its own right. Likewise, the Joker's various melodies are all appropriations of one kind or another, leaving the Bat-theme as the source of all the conventionally thematic material in the score, although the way in which Elfman scores it allows it to acquire numerous distinct significations. These include the theme as heroic signifier, the Love theme, a 'Secrets and Revelations' theme, and a Fate theme. The analysis of the use and development of the Bat-theme through the course of the film will be discussed largely in terms of these four ideas.

Other musical issues in the overall architecture of the film are sometimes more elusive. The contrast of tonal and whole-tone music is obviously a major feature of the harmonic organization, but in terms of more conventional, quasi-symphonic ideas of harmonic structure, the fact that it is in the nature of the Bat-theme to shift constantly from one key to another means that it is hard to perceive an overarching structure to how the harmony is moving in the film overall. Nonetheless, there are some clear patterns. For example, the tonal center of cues using the Bat-theme or Bat-theme-derived material often shifts downward by tone and semitone steps, and up or down by major and minor thirds, while modulations to the dominant or subdominant are rare. The Love theme occurs almost exclusively in C major, the main exception being "Tender Batcave." Here, its opening emphasizes chords of C major but is, in fact, in G major, although has reached C by the end. The Bat-theme occurs in practically every minor key available, as well as occasionally appearing in major keys, but it has a 'favorite' key in C minor. This harmonic relationship reinforces the earlier observation that the thematic relationship of the Love theme and the Bat-theme acts as a metaphor for the duality of Bruce and Batman.

Although C minor is not a key that occurs in the main title, single statements of the Bat-theme in other cues occur very often in C minor, including both the Bat-theme statements in "Family—1st Bat" at the start of act 1. At the end of the act, the first, second, and last statements of the Bat-theme in "Shootout" are all in this key, which supports the idea that C minor has a particular significance in Elfman's scheme.[1] This is confirmed by the fact that most of the action cues also make their initial statements of the theme in C minor, including "Rescue," "Batmobile Chase," "Batsuit—Charge of the Batmobile," "Batwing I," the first clear statement, some way into the cue, in "Cathedral Chase," and the end credits. Likewise, the statement of the Bat-theme over our first sight of the Batwing after the Joker releases his poison gas in "Batwing IIA" is in C minor, as is the final statement of the theme at the end of the "Finale." C minor might be thought of as Batman's home key, which makes it quite logical that it is not used in the main title: one does not, after all, want to find harmonic home at the start of the film, particularly when so much of the narrative is about Batman 'finding himself' romantically and socially.

Although harmony has a definite role to play in the score, the major structuring feature of Elfman's musical architecture is the differences in the way that the Bat-theme is used in the course of the film. In the same way that the musical similarities and differences between Batman and the Joker can be traced in relation to the act structure, so too can the uses of the Bat-theme.

Act 1: Establishing the Bat-Theme

The main title cue of any film is likely to be of significant importance: its music and images mark a boundary that separates the real world from the diegesis of the narrative. The opening credits are "like a passport into the world of the film, . . . [an] invitation to imagine."[2] The main title is the first and, potentially, the most important point at which the character of this world is established, music and image creating a specific impression as part of the contract that the film makes with its audience during the first few minutes, establishing the 'terms and conditions' of the narrative.

This is precisely the function of the main title of *Batman*. Main titles usually contain a variety of culturally coded messages concerning the narrative about to unfold, often matching musical genres to filmic ones. Militaristic music, typically using march tempos and brass-dominated orchestration, is the usual musical territory of action-adventure and superheroes. This is a film music genre firmly established by John Williams and his scores for *Superman*, *Star Wars*, and the *Indiana Jones* trilogy but substantially adapted and altered by Elfman, as discussed in chapter 4.

The main title is divided into four sections with a brief coda, outlined below (see table 6.1). Unlike *Superman* or *Star Wars*, in the course of its two-and-a-half-minute duration, the *Batman* main title undergoes seven, generally quite chromatic modulations.[3] Similarly, while the main titles of both of Williams's scores have more than one identifiable theme, there is only one theme used in Elfman's cue, namely the five-note Bat-theme (figure 6.1a). This theme, however, is constantly varied, used in several rhythmic permutations, and with several different melodic tails attached to the basic theme, each of which is capable of pushing it in a different harmonic direction. Section A, the slow, canonic introduction, uses the five-note theme without an additional melodic tail, and this is why it stays resolutely in B minor until bar twelve. Here the first tail is appended, a slip to the augmented fourth harmonized with C♯ major (figure 6.1b). What this implies is that the music will modulate to the dominant, F♯ minor but, almost without exception, this classic and conventional tonic-to-dominant modulation fails to occur, not just here but throughout the score. Instead, the usual harmonic consequence is that the tonal center reverts back to the key it started in. Williams's superheroes themes place particular importance on tonic-dominant relationships, most notably in the melodies of the themes themselves, and the tonic-dominant pairing might be read as a metaphor for the hero as straightforwardly stable. Elfman's avoidance of tonic-dominant

Table 6.1: Structure of the Main Title

Section	Tempo	Bars	Duration	Key
A	MM70	1–14a	0'00"–0'48"	B minor
B	MM146	15–34	0'48"–1'19"	B minor → A minor → G minor → F♯ minor → D minor
C	"faster"	35–66	1'19"–2'08"	G minor → C♯ minor
D		67–78	2'08"–2'22"	E♭ minor
Coda		79–82*	2'22"–2'30"	dim⁷ leading to whole tone cluster

* *The bar numbers in the score are in fact 82–85, as the preceding four bars were cut from the final recording.*

Figure 6.1: Bat-Theme Permutations.
Danny Elfman, Batman *Score, "Titles"*
a) The Bat-Theme, Bars 4–5

b) Denied-Dominant Tail, Bars 9–10

c) Falling Major Second Modulation, Sharpened Sixth Tail, Bars 19–20

d) Falling Minor Second Modulation, Arpeggiated Tail, Bars 24–28

relationships melodically and harmonically therefore adds to the idea of the hero as a fundamentally unconventional and unstable figure.

There are two other melodic tails established in this first cue, both of which provide a modulation to a somewhat unexpected key. The second tail produces modulations that shift the tonal center down a major second. Where the first tail simply appends a falling semitone step to the basic five-note melody, this version reverses the order of notes at the end of the theme, sharpens the minor sixth, and then rises another semitone to what becomes the tonic of the new key (figure 6.1c). The third tail retains this reversal of the last two notes but augments the rhythm and reinstates the minor sixth. It then appends a descending arpeggio figure, which lands on the tonic of the new key, this time a minor second below the starting key (figure 6.1d).

Although these are the principal thematic variations established in this cue, there are also several other types of modulation here that further complicate the harmonic character of the music. One is relatively conventional, with a modulation from D minor to the subdominant G minor at bar 35.[4] Others are sudden, apparently unprepared shifts in key, such as the one from F♯ minor to D minor at bar 31;[5] from C♯ minor to E♭ minor at bar 67;[6] and a modulation from G minor to the augmented fourth, C♯ minor at bar 47, surprising mainly because it seems so unchromatic in context.[7] This last unorthodox 'modulation' results from Elfman finding a new solution to his denied dominant tail: from G minor, this would normally move to chord II (A major), but the C♯, the last note of the theme in G minor, simply becomes the new tonic.

The overall harmonic scheme of the cue defies description in classical harmonic terms. The A section is firmly in B minor; the tonal center of the B section tumbles downward by tone and semitone steps from B to F♯ minor, before landing in D minor; the C section is firmly in G minor for the first half and its augmented fourth, C♯ minor for the second; and the final section is resolutely in E♭ minor, which has no obvious harmonic relationship to where the cue started or, indeed, to any of the main key areas of the rest of the cue. These multiple modulations to chromatic keys are probably one of the reasons why the score is sometimes described as Wagnerian: as with Wagner's harmonic structuring of his music, Elfman uses the melodic line to control the harmonic movement rather than vice versa. In classical harmony, the underlying chord structure dictates how the melody moves: with Wagner—and Elfman—the melodic line takes precedence and the harmony falls in underneath in response to whatever the melody demands. The effect here, however, is of music in turmoil. Arguably, the music does not modulate at all: it simply shifts irrationally to a new key area. Meanwhile, the minor modality and the tendency for the melody to be carried by instruments in the lower registers—particularly brass and bassoon—give the music its darkness. The way that the melody pushes up to its highest note and then often tumbles rapidly back down, coupled with the harmonic slippage of the unpredictable modulations, create an atmosphere not only of darkness but also of passion, turmoil, surging emotions, and potential tragedy. This is music searching for harmonic home and never finding it: the cue ends on a whole-tone chord, which allows Elfman to avoid the issue of harmonic closure altogether.

The overall harmonic instability of this first cue is complemented by a subtle rhythmic instability. The main title is fixed in neither duple nor triple time and the rhythmic form of the Bat-theme alters frequently, some examples of which can be seen in figure 6.1 above. The racing *tempi*, the changes in pulse and meter, and the general failure of the theme to settle into a particular musical shape are all part of how Batman is positioned from the outset of the narrative as a problematic hero, one whose ambivalence is reflected in the instability of his musical presentation.

The previously discussed ideas of dualism present in the narrative of *Batman* are present in its score from the very opening bars, although some of these ideas of duality are only made apparent by a comparison of the written and the aural texts. The first statement of the Bat–theme is written in 4/4, but the detail of its rhythmic scoring, using tied and dotted notes, makes it sound more as if it is in 3/4 (figure 6.2).

Figure 6.2: Rhythmic Ambivalence in the Opening Bars
Danny Elfman, Batman *Score, "Titles," Bars 1–8*

Despite this ambiguity, most of sections A, B, and C are in 4/4 (occasionally, a bar will be plus or minus a beat) but section D, the E$^\flat$ minor section, moves into 3/4 as the cue builds to its climax. One of the ways in which Batman shares common musical ground with the Joker that has not been discussed in detail so far is the way that Batman's music shifts between duple and triple meters, waltz rhythms being the Joker's territory rather than the more militaristic march rhythms that we might expect of an action-superhero. The use of 3/4, especially the Strauss and "Beautiful Dreamer" waltzes, effectively codes this meter as an indicator of the irrational through association with the Joker and his actions: his 'playful' murder of Grissom, his waltzing with Vicki's photograph, his bizarre attempt at seduction in her apartment. Throughout the film, instances of Batman or Bruce's music occurring in triple time usually have some implications in relation to the darker side of his nature, Bruce's secrets, and Batman's potential to be like his enemies. In the internal working of the Bat-theme, the 3/4-meter encodes an idea of Bruce-Batman's own internal duality and battle with the irrational, and this meter becomes one of the principal signifiers of the Secrets and Revelations theme.

This idea of internal duality is also present in the visual images of the main title. The camera appears to be panning around some vast, subterranean structure, through curving caves and gullies. However, toward the end, as the music moves into the 'irrational' 3/4 meter, we move out to view the structure as a whole and discover it to be Batman's insignia, carved in stone. However, embedded within this image is a second, shadow-image. In a trompe l'oeil effect, if one reverses the foreground and background, the insignia is revealed as a grinning pumpkin head, an image echoed by the yellow and gold of the color version of the insignia. Pumpkin heads are a particular motif in Burton's work, seen throughout *The Nightmare Before Christmas* and also in several scenes in *Sleepy Hollow.* The ghoulishly grinning face of the pumpkin head embedded in the altered version of the insignia that was created for Burton's film superimposes an image of the trickster, mischief-maker, and clown over that of the superhero, as well as making a specific reference to the Joker's fixed smile. This reinforces the idea that Batman and the Joker are dangerously similar and that Batman carries within him, as within his insignia, the potential to become the enemy.

The final feature of the main title cue that indicates this internal duality is found in the last three bars. This is the end of the codalike section, where the Bat-theme is abandoned, and instead we hear a series of heavily syncopated *tutti* diminished seventh chords that end with a whole-tone cluster, thus introducing the musical idea of the whole-tone scale within the main title as an important musical idea within the score. Its function here points to Bruce-Batman's internal conflict, preventing any conventional sense of harmonic closure but, in keeping with the way the whole-tone mode signifies throughout the film, it also marks the point of transition between the abstract space of the title sequence and the concrete narrative. As with "Up Building," the whole-tone mode underscores the movement from outside to inside, from our own reality into the imaginary and clearly dangerous space of Gotham City.

The main title then initiates the musical representation of a very unusual hero, a hero unlike the cinematic heroes and superheroes that 1980s' audiences were used to seeing. His music shifts and slips, as indeed does he during the course of the narrative. In addition, the Bat-theme has a definite resemblance to the themes of several other musical texts, all of which are similarly dark. This might be interpreted as a form of strategic allusion to those texts; or the theme might equally be read as something approaching a museme, a unit of musical meaning, where the meaning has 'something of the night' about it. Very similar themes can be heard in horror films made both before and after *Batman*. These include *The House of the Seven Gables* (score by Frank Skinner, 1940), *Hellbound: Hellraiser II* (Christopher Young, 1987), and the horror spoof *The 'Burbs* (Jerry Goldsmith, 1988), while a theme so similar that one wonders if *Batman* were the temp track is heard in the end credits of *Bram Stoker's Dracula* (Wojciech Kilar, 1992). Likewise, there is a strong similarity to the theme set to the words "*Lux aeterna dona eis*" in the main title of *Interview with the Vampire* (1994), a replacement score written at short notice by Elliot Goldenthal shortly before he wrote the music for *Batman Forever* (1995) and plausibly influenced by Elfman's *Batman* score, reinforcing the connection between *Batman* and the horror genre. There are doubtless other examples, but one of the earliest and best-known must be a song using the same five-note theme, Irving Berlin's "Let's Face the Music and Dance" (1936). With its references to both the moon and to an approaching conflict, the use of the five-note theme indicates that this romantic song is nonetheless about dangers that lurk in the night. In fact, given the Joker's interest in dancing, the Berlin song neatly summarizes some of the key narrative themes of *Batman*.

While it is not suggested that Elfman had any specific intention of alluding to this song in his music, nonetheless his theme successfully taps into a wealth of musical meanings connected to dangers lurking in the dark, particularly in horror narratives, and this is highly apposite. What, after all, is Batman if not the vampire as superhero? His transformation from man to 'bat' mirrors Dracula's famous metamorphosis and, like a vampire, he is a nocturnal creature. Even his cape mimics the iconography of Dracula as much as it does the wings of a bat. In fact, in the opening section of *Batman,* there are no less than five separate references to the possibility that Batman is a vampire: the muggers' rooftop conversation when one recounts how there was no blood left in the corpse of one of the alleged victims; Eckhardt's sarcastic comment on the muggers having seen a "giant, menacing supernatural form"; Knox's own comment to Eckhardt, "they say he can't be killed, they say he drinks blood"; the greeting Knox receives as he arrives at the news office, "well, welcome, Count Dracula," delivered in a mock-Romanian accent; the picture then produced by a fellow reporter of an anthropomorphized bat in a suit that Knox declares needs "a little more gore under the fangs"; and this is without mentioning the general association of Batman and Gotham with the gothic, the vampire being a familiar figure in nineteenth-century gothic fiction. Although present in the dialogue and images of the earliest part of the film, this is an idea that is then quickly suppressed, but the gothic vampire image persists within *Batman* in the precise contours of the theme and its associations.[8]

Having been very firmly established in the main title, the theme is clearly present in the rest of act 1 but somewhat constrained—it occurs in six of the nine cues in this section of the film although it rarely dominates a cue and usually occurs as a single statement, surrounded by other material. Thus, it emerges out of passages of string *tremolandi* in "Family—1st Bat," and out of otherwise whole-tone music at the end of "Roof Fight." This supports a reading of the opening of the film in which we technically do not know who Batman really is; nor do we know whether he is operating outside the law or fighting to uphold it. He remains a literally shadowy figure: his motif appears and disappears as swiftly and enigmatically as he does himself. In fact, single statements of the basic five-note theme are usually explicitly linked to the appearance and disappearance of Batman in both of these cues and, for the most part, in "Shootout." However, "Shootout" and "Batzone" both introduce ideas other than the Gothic heroic identity of the main title. "Batzone" introduces the theme of Secrets and Revelations, while "Shootout" introduces the Fate theme.

The idea of secrets and mystery permeates the narrative of *Batman*. The most obvious secret, the one being kept from other characters in the film, is Batman's true identity, but parallel to this runs a connected secret, something that is hidden from both characters and audience for much of the film: how did Bruce become Batman in the first place? Bruce Wayne's secrets lie at the heart of his dysfunction, his inability to have normal relationships, his inability to conform to normative behaviors, and his tendency, therefore, to don his concealing cape and mask and engage in all manner of risky behavior. It is Bruce's secrets that have led to him becoming like his enemy, violent, risk-taking, existing within society but not truly part of it. Musically, as triple-time meters are one of the main signifiers of Batman's enemy, the Joker, it makes musical sense that triple-time meters should become one of the main signifiers of the secrets that have made Bruce most like him.

The Secrets and Revelations theme can be identified in three linked cues, one occurring in each act, and each one involving both Bruce Wayne and Vicki. Vicki's presence adds an extra dimension to this group of cues—the secrets involved are both ones that she must discover if her relationship with Bruce is going to work. All the Secrets cues are ultimately linked not by the discovery of Batman's identity but by the sequence of events that leads to uncovering the truth as to his origins, the death of Bruce's parents at the hands of Jack Napier.

"Batzone" occurs immediately after Vicki and Knox's conversation with Bruce in the armory at Wayne Manor. Bruce has just left them, having been alerted by Alfred to Commissioner Gordon's sudden departure. Bat-theme scoring in 3/4 first occurs toward the end of the main title and "Batzone," occurring some twenty minutes later, is both the first cue since the main title to make use of the Bat-theme beyond a single statement, and the first exclusive use of 3/4 in a cue. It occurs in act 1 at a point when the Joker does not exist and so his relationship to waltzes has not been established. Therefore, although the meanings generated in this cue can be read in the wider context of the film as an aspect of Batman and the Joker's duality, at this point they are internal to the Bat-theme itself. As a result, 3/4 in this context gains an association with clandestine behavior, secrecy, and spying, all things that cast Bruce in a dubious light.

Thematically, the cue is based on the sharpened sixth melodic tail (see figure 6.1b). It starts with an inverted version of this in the horns (figure 6.3), the reversal acting as a musical pun that 'reflects' the fact that Vicki and Knox are looking into a mirror as they comment on whether it should perhaps be Bruce Vain rather than Wayne. The camera pans back to reveal the mirror and then the shot itself reverses, taking us through to the other side of the mirror where the CCTV camera that is watching them is revealed. Although the music at this point is tonal, this transition from one side of the mirror to the other is, in keeping with the general coherence of its use, accompanied by a falling whole-tone melody from the flute that simultaneously suggests a retrograded—mirror-imaged—Bat-theme (figure 6.4).

There is an overall sense of unease in this cue, indicative of the fact that what is occurring visually is all about forms of voyeurism, with Vicki and Knox peering into Bruce's life, while Bruce monitors the activities and conversations of his guests. The sharpened sixth melodic tail from the main title is varied for this cue, with the final note also sharpened, to end the motif on a major chord a semitone lower than the starting key (figure 6.5), although the resulting modulations are as unconventional as in the main title itself. The key of the music is constantly shifting and because of this it is sometimes unclear what key could accurately be described as the tonic: arriving on an E major chord, it is as reasonable to consider this the new tonic as it is to consider it a

Figure 6.3: Inverted Bat-Theme.
Danny Elfman, Batman *Score, "Batzone," Bars 1–2*

Figure 6.4: Whole-Tone Flute Melody.
Danny Elfman, Batman *Score, "Batzone," Bars 10–12*

Figure 6.5: Bat-Theme with Sharpened Seventh.
Danny Elfman, Batman *Score, "Batzone," Bars 15–19*

preparation for a move to A major or minor—which, of course, does not occur. The harmonic movement recalls the denied-dominant tail in this respect, in that major chords tend to behave as chord II to the minor key that follows. Harmonically, the chords shift downward by alternating minor and major semitone steps, often using the mediant of each chord as a harmonic pivot to shift, for example, from F minor to E major around the enharmonic A♭ and G♯, the unsettled harmony aiding the sense of unease (figure 6.6). As soon as any possible tonic is reached, the melody starts to push it into yet another direction with continuous canonic entries of the theme passing between brass, strings, and woodwind sections. Like the main title, the constantly shifting theme never settles, although Elfman finds a different mechanism for avoiding a sense of closure at the end: "Batzone" finishes in musical midsentence, segueing into the establishing shot of Axis Chemicals.

Figure 6.6: Reduction of Harmonic Movement in "Batzone"
Danny Elfman, Batman *Score, "Batzone," Bars 15–37*

In the same way that the Secrets theme is represented by a small but distinct group of cues, so the Fate theme is found in a small number of cues in very specific parts of the film, the end of acts 1 and 3. It could, in fact, be just as accurately described as the 'falling from a great height' theme as this describes the moments when it is used. It is, therefore, connected to the idea of the Fall, Lucifer's fall from grace after being cast out of heaven, a powerful Western symbol of fate, loss, and doom. The Fate moments and the musical idea associated with them in the film are central to the conflict between Batman and the Joker, the role that Batman played in the creation of the Joker, and the extent to which each is potentially the other's nemesis, a fate that they themselves helped to create.

The Fate motif is first heard in "Shootout." A characteristic motif in this cue is a falling minor third in the horns (see figure 5.3) and this foreshadows the Fate motif itself: the falling minor third, an inversion of the first interval of the Bat-theme as used in this cue, is connected to the sequence of actions that between them lead to Jack's fall. Near the end of the cue, having already killed Eckhardt, Jack shoots at Batman and the bullet ricochets, hitting Jack himself in the face, the impact toppling him over the edge of the catwalk. The music at this point is whole-tone, but as Jack's hand grasps at a pipe running along the base of the platform, it changes back into the Bat-theme's minor-key tonality. In the passage that follows, we hear a falling whole tone played by violins in their highest register and doubled by trumpets as Batman reaches over the catwalk rail and attempts to pull Jack back to safety (figure 6.7). This falling motif, heard only briefly, is an inversion of the first interval of the main Bat-theme, and a contraction of the falling minor third heard earlier. Batman struggles to hold onto Jack, but nonetheless Jack falls—did he actually fall in the end, or did Batman drop him? It is, in fact, impossible to be certain, although later it is clear that the Joker is convinced that he was dropped. As Jack falls, the music reverts to whole-tone music: this is both a dangerous space and also a boundary, the point of transition between Jack and the Joker. Nonetheless, that brief moment when we hear the falling whole tone—itself a potential boundary between the heroic Bat-theme and the dangerous whole-tone scale—is an important moment both musically and narratively, and both come back to haunt Batman in the final act.

Figure 6.7: Fate Motif.
Danny Elfman, Batman *Score, "Shootout," Bars 182–185*

The other element of the Fate theme is heard right at the end of act 1: as we see Jack's ruined hand emerge from beneath the water, a bell chimes ominously. This is a 'Hand of Fate' gesture, both visually and musically: the bell acts as a musical symbol for Fate, exploiting the cultural connection between the ideas of bells, mortality, and doom as demonstrated by John Donne's Meditation XVII, famously paraphrased as "ask not for whom the bell tolls: it tolls for thee."

Act 2: Batman in Love

Act 1 establishes three important ideas in relation to the Bat-theme: its role as a heroic signifier; an adaptation that is associated with Bruce's secrets; and the use of a motif derived from the theme that is connected to the idea of Fate and implicates Batman in the creation of the Joker.

Table 6.2: Division of Cues by Character in Act 2

Batman's Bat-Theme Cues	Bruce's Love Theme Cues	The Joker's Cues
	Segue	
	Kitchen Dinner	
		Surgery
	Stair Kiss	
		Face Off
Beddy Bye	Beddy Bye	
		Roasted Dude
Vicki Spys		
Clown Attack		Clown Attack
Bruce Contemplates	*Bruce Contemplates*	
		Photos
		Joker's Commercial
		Paper Spin
		Alicia's Mask
		Vicki Gets a Gift
		Alicia's Unmasking
Rescue		
Batmobile Chase		Batmobile Chase
Street Fight		Street Fight
Descent into Mystery		
Batcave		Batcave
Paper Throw		
		Joker's Poem
Sad Pictures		
Challenge/Dream		
	Tender Batcave	

In act 2, the character of the theme and its uses change considerably as it is used in connection with two new ideas: mystery and, perhaps most importantly in this act, love.

In the course of the act there are ten cues, all associated with the Joker, which do not use the Bat-theme at all (see table 6.2) but instead use the whole-tone scale, the various appropriated musics, and the Joker's distinctive timbral idiosyncrasies. Balancing this, there are twelve cues that are based on the Bat-theme. Some of them simply occupy its sound world and may make no full statement of the theme itself, or only a single statement, as in "Clown Attack," "Street Fight," and "Batcave." These tend to be cues where the music is referring to the Joker as much as it is to Batman. In addition to this are another five cues that use the most obviously melodic Bat-theme variant, the Love theme. Some of these cues are extremely short, but the fact remains that the Love theme has a role of its own in act 2 as a separate musical entity, and its importance is also reflected by the fact that it frames the act. The segue at the top of the act uses the Love theme but is astonishingly brief, and it is closely followed by "Kitchen Dinner" which, in terms of its textures, is practically identical to "Tender Batcave," the cue that eventually closes the act almost an hour later. Musically, the large-scale structure of the act is very clear: it starts with Bruce; the Joker dominates the central section; and then Batman reasserts his centrality toward the end.

Several aspects of the Love theme have already been discussed, in particular its relationship to Prince's "Scandalous," its representation of Vicki and Bruce's romance, and the contrast with the Joker's "Beautiful Dreamer." It does, however, have an additional role in the architecture of the film: apart from being associated with the theme of romance, it is also specifically associated with Vicki's discovery of Batman's identity (as opposed to disclosure of his childhood) and her role in helping him to become a more normally integrated member of society. The three cues that start the act, the segue, "Kitchen Dinner," and "Stair Kiss," establish both the melody of the theme and also the orchestration that becomes identified with Vicki herself, featuring flute, oboe, (electric) piano, and strings.

The following cue, "Beddy Bye," treats the Love theme rather differently, however. "Beddy Bye" concludes the first section of act 2, and the first half of it underscores the conclusion of the evening for Vicki and Bruce in the bedroom. The opening of the cue finds Vicki and Bruce in bed: she is asleep but he lies awake with a distinctly perplexed look on his face. Over this, we hear a very hesitant piano, an effect that might be attributed to *rubato* on the part of the pianist, but that is, in fact, fully scored by Elfman, who creates the effect by alternating between bars of 3/4 and 4/4. Seen in the wider context of the score, this alternation itself might be read as a coding of conflict between the 'positive' duple meter of the heroic Bat-theme and the 'negative' triple meter of the Secrets and Revelations idea, although this is only evident in the written text, and not a reading available from the film itself.

The piano is accompanied by strings and woodwind, so putting it clearly into the territory of the Love theme orchestration. The piano theme, however, combines the opening of the Bat-theme with a tail reminiscent of the end of the Love theme as heard in the segue (figure 6.8), suggesting a union of the two musical halves of Batman and Bruce. The melody then changes, altering the first interval to a minor second, and therefore slipping wholly into the Love theme, implying that love may have won this particular battle. The shot of the ornate clock in the bedroom indicates the passing of time and brings us back to the sleeping Vicki as a strange creaking sound wakes her. As she looks over to see Bruce hanging upside down from his frame, the motif alters again and the Love theme finds itself replaced by the first four notes of the Bat-theme. The music here outlines the conflict in Bruce between the demands of Vicki and Batman, and the omission of the next two Love theme cues, "Morning After" and "The Truth," heightens the extent to which love is deeply problematic for Bruce. After "Beddy Bye," we do not hear his Love theme again until the very end of the act, which indicates the extent to which Bruce is attempting to suppress and deny his feelings.

Figure 6.8: Love Theme and Bat-Theme Combined
Danny Elfman, Batman *Score, "Beddy Bye," Bars 2–4*

   The next musical cue is the second theme in the Secrets and Revelations group of cues, and it consolidates the connection between the Bat-theme, the 3/4 meter, and clandestine and secretive behavior initially explored in "Batzone." This time, however, positions are reversed and it is Vicki who spies on Bruce. Vicki is central to the Secrets theme: she is always present during the cues in this group and it reflects her role as journalist and photographer, someone who sees things, someone who uncovers truths. In this scene in particular, she is our eyes as we attempt to understand what Bruce is doing.
   During the cue "Vicki Spys," (*sic*) we see her following Bruce in order to learn more about him, the files of the newspaper having drawn a blank. She follows him from Wayne Manor into the city and watches him place two roses on the pavement of a back alley. The musical connections being made between "Vicki Spys" and the earlier cue rest on more than just the meter, however: the cue starts with a series of falling phrases, in particular an initial falling semitone motif very similar to the start of "Batzone"; the music is in the minor key of the Bat-theme; and it has the same lyrical, waltzlike feel. The orchestration is also remark-

ably similar, with relatively little use of brass in either cue, and with both giving particular prominence to the flute as an important melodic instrument. This can be read as a musical reference to Vicki's presence: after "Kitchen Dinner," there is a strong connection between Vicki and orchestration that features flute, oboe, strings, and harp. However, the similarity of the orchestration in "Batzone" and "Vicki Spys" also serves to differentiate it from the much louder, brass-dominated orchestration of the heroic cues.

The orchestration of "Vicki Spys" is generally more varied than that of "Batzone," and changes in texture are used to particular dramatic effect in one section: as Bruce takes out the roses, the dynamic of the music swells with the inclusion of the brass section, but as the roses hit the pavement the texture abruptly cuts away to leave only piano, glockenspiel, and strings playing harmonics. At this point, we, like Vicki, do not know what the roses signify, and the music is not helpful. The coupling of roses with the use of strings and woodwind, already associated with Vicki and the Love theme, might imply romance, but the music-box sound of the glockenspiel undercuts this mood, the unexpected shift in texture deepening the mystery of what Bruce is doing and what he may be thinking. In Elfman's scores since *Batman*, music-box textures have often been used to evoke ideas of memory, childhood, and mystery, all usually painful memories of lost innocence rather than nostalgic ones, examples being found in *Edward Scissorhands*, *Sleepy Hollow*, and *Good Will Hunting*. All these associations are appropriate to what we later understand Bruce to be remembering at this point, the death of his parents. However, the music-box sound is also something that has previously been used in connection with the Joker at the end of "Beddy Bye," in a version of the Bat-theme that is actually very similar to the waltzlike version being used here. The music box, therefore, hints at a connection between the Joker and this street corner, but one that will not be revealed until the end of the act.

This otherwise ambivalent moment is followed by the loudest gestures in the cue, two grandiose restatements by the brass section of the falling semitone motif first heard in the opening bars that make it clear that this is a dramatically powerful rather than a tenderly romantic moment: whatever the roses signify, it is not a happy memory.

Another connection between this cue and "Batzone" is that despite being composed entirely from Bat-theme material, neither cue ever states the five-note theme in its pure form, the form in which the single statements of act 1 generally occur. Instead, we have the falling semitone motif, derived from the last two notes of the Bat-theme, as well as augmentations and diminutions of the theme. As Vicki first follows him through the streets of Gotham, we hear an augmented version that uses the minor broken chord heard in "Shootout" but then rises to the minor seventh rather than the minor sixth we would normally expect (figure 6.9a). As we leave the main street and enter the more enclosed space of the back alley, the theme contracts as well, returning to the original rising opening but then rising only to the fifth rather than the minor sixth (figure 6.9b). Again, like "Batzone," the ending lacks a strong sense of closure, the final, rising phrase bringing the cue to an end on the dominant (with an added major sixth) rather than the tonic.

Figure 6.9a: Augmented Bat-Theme
Danny Elfman, Batman *Score, "Vicki Spys," Bars 11–12*

Figure 6.9b: Contracted Bat-Theme
Danny Elfman, Batman *Score, "Vicki Spys," Bars 19–21*

Figure 6.10: Bat-Theme Waltz Variation in "Vicki Spys"
Danny Elfman, Batman *Score, "Vicki Spys," Bars 36–38*

"Vicki Spys" is followed almost immediately by "Clown Attack," which, like "Shootout," makes constant allusion to the Bat-theme but generally avoids stating it fully, with the exception of the waltzlike version discussed in relation to the Joker (see figure 5.8). However, its proximity to "Vicki Spys" makes more apparent the fact that this melodically extended version of the Bat-theme can also be read in the context of the Secrets and Revelations theme as it is, unmistakably, the last version of the Bat-theme in 3/4 heard in "Vicki Spys" (figure 6.10). In "Clown Attack," therefore, it can be seen as pointing to the moment of revelation in which Bruce learns the Joker's secret identity: he recognizes him as Jack Napier, even though no one else appears to do so.

In "Bruce Contemplates/Photos," the first section of the cue is part of the Love theme group, although the Bat-theme rather than the Love theme melody is used: the music attempts to make a statement of the Love theme but ultimately fails, producing instead an approximation of the Bat-theme in its place. Nonetheless, the orchestration evokes Vicki, the object of Bruce's contemplation. At this point, however, he is contemplating the impossibility of his relationship with her and the Love theme melody is missing, although the 'sound' of Vicki remains in the use of piano, oboe, and strings.

At the end of the Joker's "Photos" section of the cue, another echo of "Vicki Spys" and the Secrets and Revelations theme occurs when we hear a roughly triple-time statement of the Bat-theme in the familiar timbres of Vicki's usual orchestration.[9] We cut from the Joker dancing with Vicki's photograph to Vicki herself phoning Knox to find out about the significance of the street corner where she observed Bruce. Again, as in "Vicki Spys," the triple-time feel of the meter can be read as an indicator of the clandestine nature of her actions.

Thus far in act 2, we have not set eyes on Batman: the narrative of the act up to this point has been largely concerned with establishing the love story and then problematizing it, first with Bruce's anxieties and secrets, and then with the Joker's interest in Vicki. Vicki's date at the museum with Bruce turns out to be a date with the Joker, but her earlier phone call has alerted Bruce to the fact that there may be a problem, although one does wonder how he knew it was the Joker who was behind it. If it were a simple misunderstanding on Vicki's part, turning up in full Bat-gear might be viewed as overkill. However, Vicki is, indeed, in danger, and this provides Batman with his first heroic opportunity.

"Rescue" is the first up-tempo Bat-theme cue since the main title. All the other uses of the Bat-theme have either been embedded in other material, as in "Shootout," or have been exploring nonheroic significations, as in "Batzone" and "Vicki Spys." Here, at last, we return to the 'Dark Knight' and the heroic signifier of the main title. The cue comes as a musical antidote to the whole-tone, harmonically ambivalent music of the previous four cues: "Rescue" starts with a quite uncharacteristic series of tonic-dominant chords as Batman suddenly crashes through the glass roof of the museum. The orchestration as he effects the rescue of Vicki is much denser than that of the main title, with massed brass carrying the melody, and strings and woodwind hammering out a rapid triplet accompaniment, the intense and regular pulse lending it a quasi-militaristic sound. The tempo is faster than the main title, at MM167:

this is an even more energetic version of the Bat-theme, although it uses the same melodic tails, shifting the tonal center of the music in ways familiar from the main title. "Rescue" unequivocally restates the Bat-theme as a heroic musical idea, and this then continues through "Bat-mobile Chase," where the Bat-theme competes with whole-tone music as Batman competes with the Joker's henchmen.

After the Batmobile is brought to a halt, the Bat-theme returns but is then repeated in a whole-tone version (figure 6.11). This propels the music into the whole-tone mode as Batman and Vicki are forced to take to the streets, the shift of tonality reflecting the way that they are forced out of the safety of the Bat-space into a dangerous Joker-space. In fact, throughout the film, the streets are dangerous and appear to belong to the Joker and the criminal element—Batman's environment is higher up where the Gothic architecture of the city is visible in the cornices and gargoyles. The Joker wants control of the streets, where the people are, whereas the more solitary Batman exists on the rooftops and in the air. Batman and Vicki are in the Joker's environment at this point in "Batmobile Chase" and, as they run, so the whole-tone music chases them. The Bat-theme only returns as they use Batman's gadgetry to ascend from the street. "Batmobile Chase" is a more equivocal state-ment of Batman's heroic identity than "Rescue": his theme is musically threatened by the whole-tone scale, and the fact remains that while in "Rescue" he was behaving in a classically heroic manner, saving Vicki from the villain, now he is engaged in the somewhat less heroic activity of running away.

Figure 6.11: Bat-Theme and Whole-Tone 'Echo'
Danny Elfman, Batman *Score, "Batmobile Chase," Bars 37–40*

Following directly on from the chase sequence in Gotham, Vicki is taken on a journey into the unknown as she finds herself truly alone with Batman for the first time. Visually, the scene accompanied by "Descent into Mystery" is a rather dull one, in which she and Batman drive through a forest and, if one takes one's attention away from the soundtrack, it must be admitted that the Batmobile looks slightly shaky. In the early part of the sequence it appears to be bouncing along the road at a fairly sedate speed, and the sense of pace and the excitement in the scene come from the music far more than the visual images.

"Descent into Mystery" is, without doubt, one of the best-known and most important cues in the score. It occurs very close to the mid-point of the film and takes the Bat-theme into completely new melodic, harmonic, and timbral areas. Two of the most obviously new features of the theme's treatment are the use of voices and the cue's absolutely harmonic stability. Whereas one of the main characteristics of the Bat-theme treatment so far has been its harmonic unpredictability, this cue starts and ends in D minor without any harmonic deviations. Instead, the musical impetus of the cue lies in the way Elfman continually varies and builds the complexity of the texture, layering the instruments and voices over a stable harmonic bass.

The use of voices is unusual in context: although many of Elfman's scores make use of voices, *Edward Scissorhands* and *Batman Returns* among them, this is the first time in *Batman* that we have clearly heard a choir. Voices are indicated in the score at the end of the slow, opening section of the main title, but they are very low in the mix of sound and might easily be missed altogether when watching the film, although they are more prominent on the soundtrack recording. The choir's unexpected and very prominent introduction into the foreground of the music this late in the score heightens the impact of the cue and indicates that there is something particularly important happening here: it has required new musical materials in order to be realized.[10]

Elfman's evocation of "O Fortuna" from Orff's *Carmina Burana* in the staccato phrasing of "Descent" lends the music a sense of the scale and power of that work (figure 6.12).[11] The words are indistinct and are not given in the score but appear to be a combination of solfège and Latin—the only clear phrase is "*in sancto*," which we hear several times. The Latinate text gives the music an impression of ritual and of mystery, exploiting the cultural association between words sung in Latin, religious rituals, *Carmina Burana*, and horror films, such as *The Omen* (1976), that have used and increased those musical associations. If the main title makes reference to a museme associated with horror narratives, the use of voices singing in Latin heightens the sense of the arcane and the occult in relation to the Bat-theme. In addition to this ritual element in the vocal writing, the instrumental writing is built on an ostinato pattern that, on one level, recalls the Bat-theme through its insistence on the intervals of the minor third and major second, but which also bears a distinct resemblance to the *Dies Irae* (figure 6.13), a musical found-object that has long been made use of by filmmakers and composers for its allusion to the day of judgment.[12] The *Dies Irae* motif acts as an ostinato throughout much of the cue, and the audible process of layers being built on top of this further increases its ritualistic sound.

Figure 6.12: "O Fortuna" Allusion
Danny Elfman, Batman *Score, "Descent into Mystery," Bars 5–6*

Figure 6.13: Dies Irae *Allusion*
Danny Elfman, Batman *Score, "Descent into Mystery," Bar 3*

All this might again be thought of in terms of Vicki and how she is 'hearing' Batman. Just as the underscore in "Batcave," the cue immediately following this one, suggests that she is hearing him as no different from the Joker, so here the music can also be interpreted as her point of view, perceiving Batman as something mysterious and probably very dangerous. This music is also one of the most powerful statements of Batman as a heroic figure that the score has allowed so far: the cue is relentless in the way it drives forward through dense layers of musical activity, unified by the absolute stability of the harmony and the regularity of the rhythmic phrases (figure 6.14). In direct contrast to the instability and unpredictability of previous Bat-theme cues, the music here speaks of control, coherence, and inexorable purpose: Batman is, without doubt, utterly in command of the situation in this scene, although his motives remain a mystery to Vicki. At the same time, the complexity of the layers, the scale of the orchestration, and the inclusion of the choir imbue Batman with an awesome and not entirely reassuring sense of authority. This is Batman as hero, fully empowered as the site of narrative agency, but the sheer magnitude of the music, the ritualistic elements, and the horror film references come close to making him Batman-as-monster. We see him at his most frightening and inhuman, actively maintaining his difference, his Otherness, through his refusal to answer Vicki's questions or even to allow her to look at him. Vicki, the character who sees, is prevented from seeing Batman: he turns on a light that dazzles her when she tries to look too closely.

Figure 6.14: Musical Layers over the Dies Irae *Ostinato*
Danny Elfman, Batman *Score, "Descent into Mystery," Bars 11–12*

Another aspect of this cue is that although its tonality and its motifs can all be traced back to the Bat-theme, once again, the five-note theme itself is largely absent. There are only two clear statements of the theme. One, a slightly augmented statement from the brass, appears right at the end as the Batmobile comes to a halt in the Batcave. The other is approximately halfway through, at the point where a sudden swell in the orchestral volume accompanies a shot of Batman pressing his foot on the gas pedal. The Bat-theme is then heard over a shot of the Batmobile hurtling toward the camera. It works as a kind of Doppler effect—the ascending first four notes have the Batmobile approaching, while the fifth note, which descends, is cued to the moment that the shot reverses, so now we see the back of the Batmobile speeding away. This Doppler effect acts as a kind of mickey-mousing, a musical substitution for a sonic phenomenon that is not present in the foley.

The last section of the cue builds to suitably gothic proportions. Recovering from being dazzled, Vicki shrieks as she realizes that they are about to crash into a rock face: instead, they pass through it and into a tunnel carved out of the solid rock. As Vicki looks back, she sees the tunnel behind them glowing red in the taillights. Accompanying this, choir and orchestra hammer out a repeating rising semitone motif, utilizing the inverted fourth and fifth notes of the Bat-theme, which therefore inverts the falling semitone motif heard in "Vicki Spys." There, the falling semitone is connected to Bruce's secrets, secrets that render him vulnerable. The rising semitone here is the counter to that vulnerability, and represents Batman's terrifying power and control over his environment (figure 6.15). Again, it is the scale, volume, and insistence of the orchestration, particularly the use of the voices, that makes this the most terrifying moment in the cue, the images supporting the idea that Vicki is being driven into hell by a monstrous, demonic Batman, the cue and the car finally coming to a halt with a conclusive statement of his theme.

Figure 6.15: "Terrifying Power" Motif
Danny Elfman, Batman *Score, "Descent into Mystery," Bars 42–43*

The economical use of the Bat-theme in "Descent into Mystery" is a clear example of the way Elfman prevents the audience from feeling bludgeoned by his theme, an adept musical solution to what might have otherwise been the problem of an essentially monothematic score. The insistence on the familiar intervals of the Bat-theme—the minor and major seconds and minor third, all used both ascending and descending in every layer of the cue (see figure 6.14)—means that the theme is being constantly evoked without having to be stated, allowing it to be kept for particular moments when it can appear out of the texture of the score, its impact not dulled by overuse.

The final section of act 2 returns to two of the narrative threads of the act and its musical themes, the Love theme and the Secrets and Revelations theme. "Sad Pictures" is a very brief cue that refers back to the Love theme in the same way as "Bruce Contemplates," and also anticipates the music of the following cue. The Love theme is not present, but the tempo and, to some extent, the orchestration associated with it are. We only hear strings, a gently moving though rather more melancholy texture than the usual wash of color that underpins the theme—an oboe is indicated in the score, but is not audible in the film, and this instead suggests a certain intentional distancing of the cue from the Love theme, although the narrative links are clear. Where before, Bruce contemplated the impossibility of his relationship with Vicki because of who he is, now Vicki starts to uncover the truth about him, a process that will lead to her being able to reconcile the existence of Batman as part of Bruce. At the end, the Bat-theme is heard clearly from the cello, with a Vickiesque flute above, a uniting of the low, dark timbres of the Bat-theme with Vicki's orchestration: she has discovered that his parents died on the street corner where she spied on him and now, understanding the trauma of the child, the ground is effectively prepared for her to accept him as Batman.

"Challenge/Dream" is the penultimate cue of act 2 and, like "Sad Pictures," it doubles another earlier cue, "Descent into Mystery." "Descent" creates a sense of Batman as gothic hero-monster, the 'Dark Knight,' heroic but dangerous. In the scene where the origin of his monstrousness—his mystery—is finally revealed, we return to the music of mystery that "Descent" established, but now it is deconstructed, its stability undermined, its layers fragmented. It is as if "Descent into Mystery" were the protecting edifice of power that Batman has built around himself, and which he refuses to let Vicki penetrate. In "Challenge/Dream," the edifice audibly crumbles, robbing Batman of the power it previously gave him, revealing instead the defenseless child he used to be.

Like "Descent," this is tonally stable, although now in A minor rather than D, and there is again a prominent piano ostinato. However, rather than the *Dies Irae* motif of the earlier cue, this is a tonic pedal note, and as such it equally evokes Jack Napier and the irregular, stuttering piano ostinato of "Jack vs. Ekhart." In "Descent," the sense of Batman's power was built through the inexorable piling of layer upon layer of musical texture. Here, the music is sparse, stripped, the ostinato and stable harmonic bass still evident but nonetheless threatened: above it, horns play a sustained dominant pedal that ends abruptly with a brief but tonally disruptive and chromatic deviation (figure 6.16a), the first clear crack in the edifice. This characteristic semitone rise alludes to the Terrifying Power motif of "Descent" (see figure 6.15) and also recalls the prominence of the same interval, in the same key, heard in the previous cue, "Sad Pictures" (figure 6.16b): there we saw only photographs of the past event, but now we are about to witness the event itself.

Figure 6.16a: Horn Motif
Danny Elfman, Batman *Score, "Challenge/Dream," Bars 3–4*

Figure 6.16b: String Motif
Danny Elfman, Batman *Score, "Sad Pictures," Bars 1–2*

Figure 6.17: Palindromic Figure
Danny Elfman, Batman *Score, "Challenge/Dream," Bars 5–6*

The cellos enter with a new motif, not unlike the types of patterns being used in "Descent." However, where that used repeating patterns to build constantly to new heights of intensity, this literally goes in musical circles, perfectly palindromic (figure 6.17). Again, as in "Descent," the

Bat-theme is evoked but not stated. Apart from the palindrome, which clearly both evokes and avoids it, a consistent melodic idea is a rising and falling figure between E and F, which would be the fourth and fifth notes of the Bat-theme in this key. Where the rising semitone alludes to the Terrifying Power motif, the falling semitone connects back to "Vicki Spys," where we heard a distinctive falling semitone figure as Vicki watched Bruce laying two roses on the street corner where his parents died. These two ideas are now linked specifically for the first time: the rising and falling semitones bring together Bruce's terrifying superheroic alter ego with the events that occurred on that street corner, and juxtaposes them with Bruce's contemplation of the image of the Joker.

As the scene moves into the "Dream" section—Bruce's memory of his parents' death—the oboes, clarinets, and synthesizer all bend their pitches downward, signaling that we are entering a different and more precarious sonic space: we are no longer in the 'real' world but inside Bruce's memory. The piano becomes more erratic, increasingly resembling the very low-pitched, aggressive piano ostinato of "Jack vs. Ekhart": Jack is part of this memory, and the music anticipates his appearance. As we see Bruce as a boy with his parents, the choir re-enters with the women's voices prominent, one of the first examples in any of Elfman's scores of the connection between upper register voices and ideas of memory and mystery. Not only does this create another connection back to the presence of voices in "Descent" but again it lends a religious and ritual aspect to the scene. The expressions on the family's faces are happy but the music is tragic and the vocal lines, with their suspensions and resolutions, recall the polyphonic texture of a mass—a requiem mass, because having shared Vicki's discovery of Bruce's childhood, we watch this scene as Bruce does, knowing that his parents will die. The music is also reminiscent of Barber's *Agnus Dei*, the vocal setting he made of his *Adagio for Strings*. This piece of music holds a particular place in the American psyche as a national hymn of mourning, used during the funerals of both Roosevelt and Kennedy, and the allusion to the *Adagio* in Elfman's score further enhances the sense of this music as a requiem.[13] The texture also connects to the strings in "Sad Pictures," which show a similar use of suspensions as part of the evocation of Bruce's tragedy.

Pitch bends are used to mark the transitions between sections of the cue. The first pitch bend occurs as we move from the present to the past; the second occurs as we move from the last happy memory into the moment of the murder itself. Each time, the downward trajectory of the pitch bends takes us further down into the tragedy, further into Bruce's secrets. The sound design of the murder scene creates echoes and distortions that connect sonically to these pitch bends, although the murder itself is unscored. This is the lowest, darkest point of Bruce's narrative: there can be no music here to mediate it.

The pitch-bending then reverses as the gun is turned on Bruce and the music comes back in: Elfman scores an upward cello *glissandi* as Bruce remembers what he came 'down here' to remember, that the man with the gun was the young Jack Napier, delivering his macabre catch-phrase. Having sunk all the way down into this memory, the music now takes us up and back out. The strings take over, still alluding to the texture of the *Adagio* and coming to an inconclusive cadence as Alfred appears with Vicki.

As the act begins with Vicki and Bruce, so it ends: Alfred, we are led to assume, has told Vicki the truth, and she comes to confront Bruce in the Batcave. "Tender Batcave" completes the romantic story line that runs through act 2 and, at the same time, acts as a partner to "Batcave," a connection that can be inferred from the title. Whereas before the music connected Batman to the Joker, now it signals a resolution of the problem of letting Vicki know the truth. She already does, and the use of the Love theme in this scene allows a merging of Bruce and Batman: the music is Bruce's but the environment is Batman's and his clothing, as mentioned in chapter 3, is atypical of both characters. This, then, is potentially someone else, a new, integrated Bruce-Batman. He has solved the mystery of his parents' death and found a woman who can accept the strangeness of his double life.

"Tender Batcave" provides the fullest exploration of the Love theme and brings in a number of ideas from other areas of the score. It revisits the orchestration associated with the theme and with Vicki and, whereas the oboe was removed from the music in "Sad Pictures," it has been added to "Tender Batcave," clearly audible despite the fact that it does not appear in the score. The cue it alludes to most strongly in terms of its orchestration is the cue that opened the act, "Kitchen Dinner," but where that was harmonically very static, rocking from one chord to the next but never moving away from its tonal center of C major, "Tender Batcave" is contrastingly chromatic. To begin with, like "Kitchen Dinner," it rocks between chords of B minor and C major, although the tonal center is G major. However, there is then an abrupt chromatic shift to G♯ minor and F major as the two chords underlying the melody and, as in other cues, when abrupt shifts such as this occur, it is highly unclear what key could reliably be described as the tonic. This kind of chromatic movement is something associated with the Bat-theme, not the Love theme, and so it appears that in the harmonic structure of the cue, the Bat-theme's unsettled, questing nature is integrated into the Love theme.

Another shift in the harmony settles into an alternation between chords of E minor and F major, with C major now becoming the tonic, the same key in which the Love theme was first explored in "Kitchen Dinner." Ultimately the cue ends in this key, confirming C major as the Love theme's harmonic home. However, before this can happen, the theme goes through a series of chromatic suspensions: first a 7-6 suspension over another G♯ minor chord and then, en route back to C major, what should be a straightforward movement through G major[7] is complicated by the introduction of an E♭ (figure 6.18). Although this could be interpreted as a chromatic suspension, it produces a chord available from the whole-tone scale and thus prepares us musically for what occurs next. As Vicki asks Bruce "I've just got to know, are we going to try to love each other?" the music slips into the whole-tone mode, and the final series of chords rocks between C major and whole-tone clusters (figure 6.19). The music of the cue has prepared us for this so thoroughly, with the increasingly dissonant suspensions in the previous bars, that this movement between tonal and whole-tone chords might easily pass unnoticed and is certainly easier to grasp from the score than from the soundtrack. However, the subtle presence of the whole-tone mode is quite logical in terms of its overall signification in

Figure 6.18: A Chromatic Route to C Major
Danny Elfman, Batman *Score, "Tender Batcave," Bars 25–27*

Figure 6.19: Whole-Tone Clusters
Danny Elfman, Batman *Score, "Tender Batcave," Bars 28–31*

the score. First, we are at one of the most important structural and narrative boundaries in the film. In terms of the local narrative, this is a point of transition and decision for Bruce: he is being asked to decide where he wants his relationship with Vicki to go. Equally, this cue—and his response to Vicki's question—is the moment of transition between acts 2 and 3 and, therefore, the point of crossing into the most dangerous space of all, the final act's confrontation with the Joker. This moment is the exception to the rule that the whole-tone scale is not used for Batman in act 2 but, just as in act 1, its use here signals his ambivalence. In act 1, that ambivalence was moral; here, it is romantic. He still does not completely commit to Vicki, saying instead that he wants to try to make their relationship work but, in effect, not right now, as he has to go and face the Joker. The cue ends with an inversion of the Love theme, its opening, rising phrase recast as a somber descent. In keeping with the general pattern of the three-act structure, act 2 closes on a less than entirely optimistic note.

Act 3: Return of the Hero

The function of the third act in a film is to resolve the conflict between the two central characters, but one of the unusual aspects of *Batman* is that there are effectively two pairs of central characters with conflicts in need of resolution: Batman and the Joker, and Batman and Bruce. A resolution of both these relationships is achieved, and it is a measure of the strength of Elfman's score that in many respects the Bruce-Batman conflict, in particular, is largely resolved by means of the music. The score also underpins the series of conflicts, triumphs, and reversals that make up the main part of act 3 as Batman takes on the Joker. In terms of costume as an indicator of which character is present, technically Bruce does not appear in this act. His pursuit of the romantic narrative in act 2 must now give way to allow Batman to bring the heroic narrative to the fore.

When the act begins with "Batsuit—Charge of the Batmobile," the Bat-theme has again been absent for some time. As if to counter this absence and, certainly, to make clear that this is the final part of the story where Batman must surely be triumphant, act 3 begins with a grand affirmation of Batman's musical identity as he prepares for action in a series of iconic framing shots: the locker opening to reveal the Batsuit; the fastening of the utility belt; a shot of the Bat-symbol on Batman's chest; and then the slow raising of his head to reveal the distinctive silhouette, the climax of shot and music being the point where his eyes are revealed.

The music is similarly iconic and recalls the opening of the main title, the first in a series of musical reminders of previous Bat-theme cues. This is a heavily contracted version of the opening canonic section that goes through a process of revealing the Bat-theme, first three notes, then four, then the full five-note theme and the denied-dominant tail. The iconic status of the music is further signaled by the addition of the choir to this cue. The choir's presence timbrally connects this use of the Bat-theme to "Descent into Mystery" and the idea of Batman as a powerful, purposeful hero. The way in which the visual images focus on the suit itself as much as the man within it reflects the extent to which the gadgets, the icons of Batman's identity that are the proof of his superhero status, are strongly connected to this musical signification.

The second section of the cue, "Charge of the Batmobile," continues this process of reestablishing the Bat-theme as a heroic signifier, in one of the fullest explorations of the theme since "Batmobile Chase"—again, the gadget, this time the Batmobile itself, is the center of attention. As with "Batsuit," there is a distinct similarity to the main title, but some equally distinct differences, particularly in terms of the harmonic direction in which the music is pushed by the melodic line. In the first half of "Charge," we watch the Batmobile drive into Axis chemicals and drop its payload of bombs. The music starts in C minor, and then the denied-dominant tail is altered so that instead of ending on a chord of D major and then returning to C minor, the chord and the key shift to E♭ minor (figure 6.20). Elfman then reuses the same tail, this time landing on the expected chord of F major and then, at last, for the first time in the film, the dominant is not denied. The music modulates from E♭ minor to B♭ minor, the timing of this convincingly heroic modulation marking the point at which Batman finally starts to act to bring down the Joker.

Figure 6.20: Altered Denied-Dominant Tail
Danny Elfman, Batman *Score, "Batsuit/Charge of the Batmobile," Bars 14–17*

This then leads into the second half of "Charge," as the Batmobile drives at speed back through the now exploding chemical works. Here,

Elfman reuses the rising semitone motif from the end of "Descent into Mystery" (see figure 6.15), which reveals a paralleling of actions between those two sections of the narrative. In "Descent," it was used at the point where the car goes through the rock wall into the tunnel, lit red by the taillights, as if transporting Vicki into some hellish dimension; here it occurs as the Batmobile escapes from the exploding factory, negotiating a tunnel of flames, another hellish reference that reinforces the ascending semitone as a signifier of Batman's terrifying power and his control of his environment. However, at the last moment, it is revealed that Batman himself was never in the car and is operating it by remote control. The Joker, meanwhile, is in his helicopter, and taunts Batman before flying off to Gotham.[14]

The festival parade opens with the Joker's use of Prince's "Trust," reestablishing his sound world of appropriations in contrast to the Bat-theme. As Batman arrives on the scene, his music therefore finds itself in direct competition with the Joker's. "Batwing" is a cue in three parts, the first, "Batwing I" underscoring Batman's arrival at the parade, and the much longer "Batwing II" (parts A and B) underscoring his conflict with the Joker on Gotham's streets. The musical competition of Batman-Elfman and the Joker-Prince is the reason for the brevity of "Batwing I," as we cut from the street to the Batwing and back to the street, a series of shots that again suggests that the street is the Joker's chosen environment whereas the air belongs to Batman.

"Batwing I" continues what the previous cue began, restating and reaffirming Batman's heroic identity, with the Bat-theme being given in its home key of C minor in a rhythmic form reminiscent of the B section of the main title. It shares the distinctive, militaristic triplet snare drum accompaniment, but uses the new melodic tail from "Charge of the Batmobile" that takes the music, again, from C minor to E♭ minor. C minor continues to be important as a key for the Bat-theme, with C minor statements in "Batwing II" occurring first as Batman makes ready his weapons and again as he gets the Joker in his sights.

The use of the rising whole-tone motif in "Batwing II" has already been discussed in the previous chapter, but it is worth recalling here both for the way in which it evokes elements of "Shootout," the previous major confrontation between the two principal characters, and also for the way it symbolizes the threat the Joker poses. This is both a physical threat and also a specifically musical threat because the initial interval of the Bat-theme is being used for the Joker's actions, as if his whole-tone music were threatening to take over the Bat-theme itself.

One of the musical outcomes of "Shootout" was the introduction of the Fate theme, a major element of which is the falling whole-tone motif, and this, of course, is the inversion of the rising motif that is found throughout "Batwing II." The question that the Fate theme itself raises is 'whose fate?' At the point that the falling motif first occurs in "Shootout," the answer is clearly Jack, the character who falls, although his resurrection as the Joker reopens the question. The Joker's appropriation of the inverted motif here can be read as an attempt to counter Fate and to reassert his agency over Batman's by encroaching on the Bat-theme and threatening to subsume it into the Joker's musical territory. This becomes even more explicit at one point as the motif transforms into what is melodically the Joker's Strauss waltz variant of the Bat-theme from "Clown Attack," used here at the point that Knox tries but fails to get control of the balloons (figure 6.21). All he succeeds in doing is destabilizing the henchman to the point that they lift off into the air, beyond Knox's power to control. The Joker's likelihood of victory and, as part of that, his claim to the narrative's musical space, increases. The air, however, is Batman's element: the Joker might have been wise to have devised a more ground-based plan of attack. The Joker-coded Bat-theme is immediately followed by the true theme as Batman himself comes to the rescue, snatching back his music as he snatches the balloons out of the air and whisks them away.

Figure 6.21: Joker's Bat-Theme Appropriation
Danny Elfman, Batman Score, "Batwing IIB," Bars 60–62

Also connecting us back to "Shootout" and the theme of Fate is the use of tubular bells. In "Shootout," the chime of the tubular bell acts as a musical 'Hand of Fate' gesture. The idea of Fate and falling is again present in the use of tubular bells here: we first hear them chiming as Batman makes his steep descent into the 'canyon' of Gotham's streets, an intentional fall but just as dangerous, anticipating other falls and chimes to come. The same gesture is used again as he makes his way out of the canyon with the Joker's balloons: now it signifies a failure to rise rather than a fall and the possibility that Batwing will not be able to pull up before hitting the building at the end of the city street. The final use of the chimes comes right at the end of the cue as the previous intentional fall and the following near-miss culminate in true disaster: the Joker shoots the Batwing out of the sky and Batman crashes to the ground, the tubular bell's 'Hand of Fate' doubling an ominous, four-note Bat-theme played by the full orchestra, all in their lowest registers.

As if to confirm the Joker's victory and the success of his 'rising whole-tone motif strategy' in repositioning him as the victorious narrative agent, "Cathedral Chase" reintroduces the falling whole-tone Fate motif, associating it with the fallen and apparently defeated Batman. The cue starts as Vicki runs toward the burning Batwing: the semiquaver minor third motif mimics her footsteps and the urgency with which she seeks, but cannot find, Batman. As the Joker comes to claim her, his prize as winner of the battle, the music slips into the whole-tone mode, with Vicki's oboe outlining an angular, awkward melody—quite unlike the Love theme—over parallel organ chords that first rise and then fall by a whole tone, recalling the Fate motif and the Joker's mastery of it in the previous cue as well as anticipating what is to come (figure 6.22).

Figure 6.22: Whole-Tone Organ Chords
Danny Elfman, Batman *Score, "Cathedral Chase," Bars 13–16*

The Joker and Vicki move toward the cathedral to climb the tower. As they leave, the music shifts back into minor-key tonality, picking up the organ chords as Batman staggers from the wreckage of the Batwing. The prominent interval at this point is a falling semitone, the inversion of the Terrifying Power motif at the moment when Batman is completely disempowered: his Batwing—his all important gadgetry—is destroyed, he is clearly concussed, he has lost Vicki, and the Joker is escaping. In fact, at this point, it appears that the Joker has won: it would seem that he is Batman's nemesis after all, and the music underlines this point. As Batman disentangles himself from the wreckage and starts to head toward the cathedral, the orchestra states the Bat-theme in C minor, its favored key: the hero has returned, but there is nothing triumphant in his Bat-theme now, and a new tail, which leaps upward by a minor sixth, sounds like a cry of anguish (figure 6.23). As he stumbles into the cathedral, the sense that this has turned into a tragedy is further signaled by the reintroduction of the Fate motif itself, here given as a pair of falling whole-tone figures over a chromatically moving bass (figure 6.24).

Figure 6.23: Bat-Theme as "Cry of Anguish"
Danny Elfman, Batman *Score, "Cathedral Chase," Bars 29–30*

Figure 6.24: Fate Motif
Danny Elfman, Batman *Score, "Cathedral Chase," Bars 33–36*

For a scene that is about climbing up an astoundingly tall tower, this cue is overwhelmingly dominated by falling melodic figures, which on one level might seem like a perversely inverted mickey-mousing effect, but which reflects the degree to which the music brings out what is happening psychologically rather than visually. The visual images may be about climbing upward, but the falling gestures of the score reinforce the sense of Batman as a fallen and disempowered hero.

He staggers through the cathedral and knocks over the benches, while the Joker, calm, relaxed, and eminently in control, herds Vicki up the bell tower. In this sequence, we hear a new version of the Bat-theme that symbolizes Batman's status as fallen hero, taking the sharpened-sixth tail (figure 6.1c) and appending to it a sinking melodic tail that takes it right down to the depths of the orchestra's range (figure 6.25). A series of these tumbling Bat-theme statements ends with another indicator that the Joker is triumphant: as he kisses Vicki's dropped shoe before throwing it over the stairway banister, we hear again his appropriated Bat-theme melody from "Clown Attack" and "Batwing II," with typi-

cally Jokeresque timbral details as the shoe falls: staccato upper woodwind, glockenspiel, and celeste. The message is clear: he has control of
both Vicki and the Bat-theme.

Figure 6.25: Bat-Theme with Falling Tail
Danny Elfman, Batman *Score, "Cathedral Chase," Bars 41–46*

As Batman comes upon the fallen shoe, we hear his falling semitone
motif, the same inversion of the Terrifying Power motif heard earlier in
this cue, again appearing here as a fall from G to F# (figure 6.26), signaling Batman's loss of power and, more specifically, his loss of Vicki,
who has become a living symbol of 'to the victor the spoils' by this point
in the narrative. In the context of "Descent into Mystery," the rising
motif very specifically represented his power over Vicki at that moment,
and now, just as specifically, the inversion represents its loss.

Figure 6.26: Inverted Terrifying Power Motif
Danny Elfman, Batman *Score, "Cathedral Chase," Bars 66–67*

As the Joker climbs through the trapdoor into the belfry, the Fate
motif (see figure 6.24) returns, but over this ground bass, Elfman writes
a completely new, soaringly rhapsodic melody for the violins. This is
the moment of absolute defeat for Batman: the Joker has reached the
top of the tower, where his helicopter may arrive to take him away at
any second, and in order to assure his victory, he uses his joke-shop
flower to spray acid on the bolts holding one of the bells in place. The
violin melody completes the cue's sense of overwhelming tragedy, and
as the bell plunges down the tower, the bass simplifies to a single pair
of chords, a single falling whole tone. As the violin melody comes to a
close, the Fate motif comes to the fore, played by organ, oboe, clarinet,
and bassoon, with the rest of the orchestra on an insistent triplet pedal.

The underlying harmony of the motif constantly alters, but the two bass notes of each chord are D and A^b, the tritone connecting the music again to the whole-tone scale, confirming that Batman's defeat is the Joker's victory. The sound of the bell as it falls in this sequence connects the diegetic sound of the film to the musical soundtrack, and the previous use of tubular bells as a signifier of Fate. There is no need for chimes in this cue as they are present within the narrative itself, unifying for the first time the two elements of the Fate theme, the bell and the falling whole-tone, and reasserting the connection between the idea of fate and the idea of objects falling from a great height.

The forces of law are now prevented from involvement in the action by the bell, which blocks their route: all they can do now is watch. The Joker's ascendancy is again suggested in a series of rising triplets, the uppermost note each time being a whole tone higher than the phrase before (figure 6.27). However, now there is another reversal of fortune. Directly countering the Joker's whole-tone claim on the sonic space, Batman and the Bat-theme suddenly reemerge. Batman reappears, unscathed by the bell's fall and now moving faster, while his Bat-theme, still using the sharpened-sixth tail, no longer falls but instead finds its original ending restored. As this is played, Batman sees Vicki's coat, and the need to rescue her reenergizes him: he breaks into a run up the stairs. Outside, the police, in their role as spectators, shine lights up the cathedral tower. The cue ends with a restatement of the Bat-theme that falls and fades away—but this time it signals Batman's cautious entry into the belfry rather than suggesting his defeat.

Figure 6.27: Rising Whole-Tone Sequence
Danny Elfman, Batman *Score, "Cathedral Chase," Bars 110–111*

"Waltz" represents the last barrier standing between Batman and a confrontation with the Joker, the last instance in which their music competes with each other, and this time Batman comes out as the victor. Having defeated the henchmen, he moves finally into a direct, face-to-face confrontation with the Joker in "Showdown A." This the final cue in the Secrets and Revelations group, connected therefore to "Batzone" and "Vicki Spys." As in the other cues, Vicki is present, but this time she is with Batman rather than Bruce. However, the scene occurs after

Vicki has learned that they are the same person, and so whereas before she perceived herself as being with either one or the other, the distance between the two has now been collapsed into a single identity.

Like the previous Secrets cues, "Showdown A" is written in a triple-time meter, starting in 6/4 and later moving to 3/4. Like those other cues, initially we have recognizable but consistently incomplete statements of the Bat-theme as Batman attacks the Joker. Then, at the point that Batman explicitly states the truth that has been hidden from him since childhood, that Jack-Joker killed his parents—and at the point, therefore, that Vicki herself learns this—the full, unaltered five-note Bat-theme is introduced for the first time in the Secrets theme group, in a form very similar to the 3/4 section of the main title: canonic entries that remain harmonically stable, this time in B flat minor. Just as the use of the whole-tone scale at the end of "Showdown A" indicates a serious moral lapse at the moment that Batman attempts to kill the Joker in cold blood, so the use of the Joker's 3/4 meter for all the cues in this group underlines the ethically dangerous nature of these scenes and the secrets they conceal, leading to Bruce and Vicki spying on each other, and Bruce-Batman nearly becoming an unequivocal murderer. In fact, the Joker's role in this scene seems to be attempting to mitigate Batman's violence through a series of comic interjections, with his odd onomatopoeic exclamation as Batman throws him into the wall the first time, the ejecting of his joke-shop false teeth the second time, and the subsequent "you wouldn't hit a guy with glasses?" line, all of which seem to be trying to distract the viewer from noticing that Batman is quite intentionally trying to kill the Joker.

The lesson is perhaps that secrets are very dangerous things to keep, but maybe even more dangerous to let out. The cues that make up the Secrets group connect the key scenes in the process of Vicki and the audience learning the truth of the connection between Batman and the Joker, between Bruce and Jack. The use of 3/4 and the way that tempo is coded in the film illustrates what a difficult and dangerous process this is, while the fact that orchestration associated with Vicki predominates in these cues gestures both toward her role in seeing and therefore understanding Bruce and toward this being a process that is essential for his future happiness with her.

"Showdown A" ends with Vicki and Bruce being pulled over the side of the cathedral by the Joker. The music of "Showdown II," which picks up almost immediately, underlines this on a number of levels, with the reintroduction of the Joker's rising whole-tone motif from "Batwing II," transitions into the whole-tone mode, and use of typical Joker-coded timbres, such as flutter tongue for the flute when he slips and almost falls, and prominent use of tom-toms and xylophone. However, the coding of the music toward the Joker as victor is much more equivocal: his rising whole-tone motif is frequently paired with the falling whole-tone Fate motif, the latter effectively canceling out the triumph implied by the former. Meanwhile, Batman's actions are strongly connected to statements of the Bat-theme, first as he reaches for the Bat-bolo on his utility belt and then as he fires it to tie the Joker to the gargoyle. As the Joker's helicopter tries to pull him up and the gargoyle breaks off, its weight now hanging from the Joker's leg, the music abruptly shifts back to the falling whole-tone Fate motif. Just as before, when we heard this motif briefly at the end of act 1 as Jack hung from Batman's grip over the vat of chemicals, now we hear it again, much more forcefully, as he meets his fate for the second time. He is brought down not just by Batman but by the architecture of the city itself as represented by the gargoyle, symbolically reinforcing the connection between the Gothic Batman and Gotham. Once again, the Joker falls, and this time, there will be no return.

Batman and Vicki are, meanwhile, still hanging from a great height. Batman starts to pull them up, and a more gentle Bat-theme statement in the violins begins—but this is a false lead, and it breaks off abruptly as they fall to the same whole-tone music as the Joker a few seconds before. Fortunately, Batman is not out of gadgets yet, and they come to rest halfway down the cathedral. The gentle Bat-theme statement from the strings is allowed to complete itself this time, turning into one of the "Beddy Bye" variations, the last time that Vicki and Bruce-Batman were so intimately in each other's arms (see figure 6.8). The tender rocking of the Love theme is introduced, now serving to mimic the couple as they swing gently through the air on the end of a wire.

The finale moves beyond the local conflict that has dominated act 3, namely the defeat of the Joker, and returns to the other problem of act 2, of how Batman can exist in a way that does not render Bruce dysfunctional. There are two elements to this: first, Batman's integration into the functioning of the law within Gotham, and second, the cementing of Bruce's relationship with Vicki.

In terms of the romance, "Finale" provides a resolution of the musical problem originally presented by "Beddy Bye," namely that it only takes a semitone shift to turn the Love theme back into the Bat-theme. The Love theme starts with a minor second and the Bat-theme with a major second and this is all that prevents one being overthrown by the other, which is exactly what happens in "Beddy Bye." The finale provides a range of alternative solutions, of other ways in which the two musical themes can relate to and transform each other, a suitably optimistic metaphor for how Vicki and Bruce might approach their future relationship. These solutions include using the Love theme as a new tail to the Bat-theme itself (figure 6.28a); reversing this relationship and using the Bat-theme as an imitative echo of the Love theme (figure 6.28b); and ultimately abandoning both themes to create a new theme at the climax of the cue that combines elements of both, the major-key tonality of the Love theme with the major second interval of the Bat-theme (figure 6.28c). The finale allows Bruce and Batman's themes to integrate, to negotiate a new and triumphant form that promises a hopeful and happy future for him.

Figure 6.28a: Love Theme as Bat-Theme Tail
Danny Elfman, Batman Score, "Finale," Bars 10–13

Figure 6.28b: Bat-Theme as Love Theme Echo
Danny Elfman, Batman Score, "Finale," Bars 20–23

Figure 6.28c: Bat-Theme and Love Theme Combined
Danny Elfman, Batman Score, "Finale," Bars 37–41

Batman, meanwhile, must escape the irrationality of his dark side and mature into a fullfledged superhero and just warrior, and the finale offers him an optimistic future, too. It has been noted by numerous other listeners that at the end of the cue, as the camera pans up the building to reveal Batman silhouetted against the night sky, Elfman's music contains an unmistakable allusion to the opening section of Richard Strauss's *Also Sprach Zarathustra*. The most famous use of this piece of music in a film is found in Stanley Kubrick's *2001: A Space Odyssey* (1968), where the music is used for several sequences, including the planetary alignment sequence during the main title, and the image of the Star Child suspended in space, gazing at the earth at the end. The opening bars from Strauss's composition correspond to the prologue of Nietzsche's epic poem, in which the prophet Zarathustra sits alone at the top of a mountain and watches the sun rise, announcing the dawning of not simply a new day but of a new era, heralding the coming of the Superman, who Nietzsche saw as being the next stage in man's spiritual evolution. It is clear how this acts as a parallel and commentary on *2001*'s overall premise, and both the music and the image from Kubrick's film are alluded to in the final visual and musical images of Burton and Elfman's *Batman*. Batman, like the Star Child, is pictured against the blackness of the night sky, illuminated by the glow of the Bat-sign at which he gazes, while the music recalls the triumphant rising phrases of Strauss's score. The chiming of the tubular bell at the climax reintroduces the idea of Fate, only now it is transformed into a positive, hopeful, and heroic fate rather than the uncertain destiny that has characterized the narrative and the music before this point. As Kubrick used Strauss's music to allude to the dawning of a brave new day in the history of mankind, so Elfman's allusion refers to the dawning of a brave new night in Gotham City, guarded by not Superman but Batman, the Dark Knight himself.

Harmonically, the final bars of the finale are a dramatic contrast to the harmonic turbulence that characterized the main title. The harmonic ambivalence of the main title's whole-tone ending is also countered here: the harmony of the final bars has a classically well-formed I–IV–V–I structure, the final perfect cadence giving the cue a sense of triumphant closure that brings the combined Bat- and Love theme to its harmonic home: the final transformation ends in an unequivocal C major. However, it is then immediately followed by a restatement of the original five-note Bat-theme in C minor. Given that C major is the home key of the Love theme, and C minor the favored key of the Bat-theme, this might be read as another aspect of the link between the two: Batman's favored key of C minor is the dark twin to Bruce's C major, the two placed side by side in the concluding bars of the finale. It can be read either as an optimistic synthesis or, perhaps more credibly, as a slightly troubling reappearance of the theme at this moment. The triumphalism of the Straussian transformation is potentially undermined by the return of the old, unreconstructed theme, a suggestion that there may be more of the story to come: the music leaves the film open to a sequel. The idea that the old, more problematic Batman identity might reassert itself, despite Vicki's benign presence, is then reinforced by the end credits, which reiterate much of the main title material in terms of treatment of the theme, structure, and chromatic harmonic treatment, only now even faster and more furious.

Notes

Chapter 1

1. Randall D. Larson, "Danny Elfman: From Boingo to *Batman*," *Soundtrack!* September 1990, 20.

2. Elfman has made multiple references to the influence of these figures and films in interviews including: Paul Zollo, "Danny Elfman: Upholding Tradition (with a Sense of Humor)," *The Hollywood Reporter: Film and TV Music Special Report*, January 1989, S-57; Bob Remstein, "In Control," *New Zealand Film Music Bulletin*, August 1990, 10; Larson, "Boingo to *Batman*," 20; Didier Deutsch, "Danny Elfman Interview," *Soundtrack!* December 1993, 8–9.

3. Frederick C. Szebin and Steve Biodrowski, "Interview with Danny Elfman," *Soundtrack!* March 1997, 6.

4. Blair Jackson, "Oingo Boingo: The Band that Wouldn't Die," *Bay Area Music Magazine*, 5 December 1980, 29.

5. Robyn Flans, "Oingo Boingo: Mondo Schizo," *Bay Area Music Magazine*, 7 October 1983, 19.

6. Rick Clark, "Danny Elfman," *Mix Magazine*, May 2001, at http://mixonline.com/ar/audio_danny_elfman/ (accessed 24 October 2002).

7. Clark, "Danny Elfman," online.

8. John M. Glionna, "A Different Beat," *Los Angeles Times Magazine*, 18 April 1999, 10.

9. Jackson, "The Band that Wouldn't Die," 29.

10. See Richard Davis, *Complete Guide to Film Scoring: The Art and Business of Writing Music for Movies and Television* (Boston, Mass.: Berklee Press, 1999), 279; Clark, "Danny Elfman," online.

11. Danny Elfman, "Chimp Symphony Op. 37," *Planet of the Apes*. Twentieth Century Fox Home Entertainment, 2002. DVD.

12. Doug Adams, "Tales from the Black Side: An Interview with Danny Elfman," *Film Score Monthly*, June 1997, 23. Elfman draws a distinction between the film music composition and other forms of music composition. Partch

was as much a composer as an inventor of musical instruments but Elfman's comment indicates an awareness of different processes underlying different types of compositional activity.

13. See Christopher Willman, "Twentieth Century Schizoid Man," *Grammy Magazine,* Summer 1994, 22; Davis, *Complete Guide,* 279; Clark, "Danny Elfman," online.

14. Clark, "Danny Elfman," online.

15. Lucy Green, *How Popular Musicians Learn: A Way Ahead for Music Education* (Aldershot: Ashgate, 2001), 60–76.

16. Clark, "Danny Elfman," online.

17. Flans, "Mondo Schizo," 16.

18. The first release by Oingo Boingo was an EP simply entitled *Oingo Boingo* (1980). Their complete list of albums is: *Only a Lad* (1981); *Nothing to Fear* (1982); *Good for your Soul* (1982); *Dead Man's Party* (1985); *BOI-NGO* (1987); *Boingo Alive* (1988); *Skeletons in the Closet: The Best of Oingo Boingo* (1989); *Stay* (1989); *Dark at the End of the Tunnel* (1990); *Best o'Boingo* (1991); *Boingo* (1994); *Farewell* (1996); and the postdisbandment album *Anthology* (1999).

19. See, for example, Jackson, "The Band that Wouldn't Die"; Flans, "Mondo Schizo"; Cary Darling, "Only Eight Lads: Boingo's Difficult Teenage Years," *Bay Area Music Magazine,* 8 May 1987, 24–28.

20. Clark, "Danny Elfman," online.

21. Larson, "Boingo to *Batman,*" 20.

22. Jackson, "The Band that Wouldn't Die," 28.

23. Glionna, "A Different Beat," 10.

24. Willman, "Schizoid Man," 22.

25. Willman, "Schizoid Man," 22.

26. Adams, "The Evolution of Elfman," *Film Score Monthly,* January 1999, 21.

27. The only film Spielberg has made with another composer since 1975 is *The Color Purple* (1985) with music by Quincy Jones.

28. Dan Hassler-Forest, "The *Auteur* as Marketing Concept," *Tim Burton: Auteur or Marketing Concept? A Hypertext,* n.d., at http://www.euronet.nl/users/mcbeijer/dan/home_burton.html (accessed 12 December 2001).

29. David Hughes, *Comic Book Movies* (London: Virgin Books, 2003), 36–37. Hughes documents how the film rights to *Batman* were acquired shortly after the making of *Superman* (1978), and the film was originally due to open in 1981 but instead languished in "production hell" for the best part of a decade, before finally being given to Burton.

30. This belief is still very much in evidence: while writing this book, there have been several occasions when friends and colleagues have made comments indicating that they consider it an accepted fact that Elfman does not write his own music.

31. Robert L. Doerschuk, "Danny Elfman: The Agony and the Ecstasy of Scoring *Batman*," *Keyboard*, October 1989, 85.

32. Doerschuk, "Scoring *Batman*," 84.

33. Doerschuk's interview was printed at a time when *Keyboard* was becoming more focused on technology and popular music performance, including jazz. For almost a decade, starting in 1980, the magazine had a regular "Contemporary Piano" column that examined repertoire from Ravel and Cowell to Boulez and Berio. However, this column was discontinued in the same month that Doerschuk's interview with Elfman was printed.

34. Doerschuk, "Scoring *Batman*," 87.

35. Lukas Kendall, "Interview: Steve Bartek," *Film Score Monthly*, December 1995, 15–16.

36. Doerschuk, "Scoring *Batman*," 85.

37. Micah D. Rubenstein to *Keyboard*, January 1990, 10.

38. Rubenstein, 10

39. Danny Elfman, "An Open Letter from Danny Elfman," *Keyboard*, March 1990, 64.

40. Lukas Kendall, "Danny Elfman: From *Pee-Wee* to *Batman* to Two Films a Year," part 2, *Film Score Monthly*, December 1995, 11.

41. Kendall, "Steve Bartek," 15.

42. Kendall, "Steve Bartek," 14–15.

43. Glionna, "A Different Beat," 10.

44. Kendall, "Steve Bartek," 15.

45. Kendall, "*Pee-Wee* to *Batman*," 2: 11; Kendall, "Steve Bartek," 15.

46. Kendall, "Steve Bartek," 16.

47. See, for example, Zollo, "Upholding Tradition," S-57; Lukas Kendall, "*Pee-Wee* to *Batman*," part 1, *Film Score Monthly*, October 1995, 13; Davis, *Complete Guide*, 278; Clark, "Danny Elfman," online.

48. Glionna, "A Different Beat," 10.

49. Three of Burton's films are among Elfman's top ten box office successes: *Batman* (2); *Planet of the Apes* (6); *Batman Returns* (7). *Sleepy Hollow* was relegated to eleventh place in 2002 by the success of *Men in Black II*. See Scott Bettencourt, "*Film Score Monthly*'s Top Forty Hit Makers," *Film Score Monthly*, September 2002, 27.

Chapter 2

1. See Chapter 1, n. 47.

2. David Cooper, *Bernard Herrmann's* Vertigo*: A Film Score Handbook* (Westport, Conn.: Greenwood Press, 2001), 17.

3. Cooper, *Vertigo*, 17.

4. For Rota's influence on Elfman's score, see Randall D. Larson, "Danny

Elfman: From Boingo to *Batman*," *Soundtrack!* September 1990, 20; Lukas Kendall, "*Pee-Wee* to *Batman*," part 1, *Film Score Monthly*, October 1995, 14.

5. Joseph B. Mauceri, "Music of the Night: An Interview with Danny Elfman," *Fear Magazine*, July 1990, at http://www.geocities.com/boingo20001/fear90.html (accessed 20 October 2002).

6. Bob Remstein, "In Control," *New Zealand Film Music Bulletin*, August 1990, 10.

7. For Elfman's dislike of romantic comedy, see Rob Lowman, "The Elfman Cometh," *News Dot Com*, 5 August 2001, at http://www.angelfire.com/trek/ortreat/a15.html (accessed 24 October 2002).

8. The first reviewer to use this adjective was probably Desson Howe of *The Washington Post*, whose review of 23 June 1989, describes Elfman's score as "Gothic-rhapsodic." See Desson Howe, "*Batman*," *The Washington Post*, 23 July 1989 at http://www.washingtonpost.com/wp-srv/style/longterm/movies/videos/batmanpg13howe_a0b220.htm (accessed 20 October 2003).

9. Remstein, "In Control," 10.

10. Darkman is not a comic book character, although the film was clearly modeled on and marketed as part of the comic book superhero genre of films.

11. These words are among those particularly identified in Bill Engelhardt and Jeff Bond, "The Never Ending Style Discourse," *Film Score Monthly*, 27 August 1997 at http://www.filmscoremonthly.com/articles/1997/27_Aug---Style_discourse.asp (accessed 1 May 2003).

12. See, for example: Mauceri, "Music of the Night," online; Larson, "Boingo to *Batman*," 25; Daniel Schweiger, "Danny Elfman Returns," *Soundtrack!* September 1992, 17; Didier Deutsch, "Danny Elfman Interview," *Sound-track!* December 1993, 9.

13. Danny Elfman, liner notes for Danny Elfman, *Music for a Darkened Theater: Film and Television Music*, volume 2, MCA Records compact disc MCAD2-11550.

14. Andy Dursin, "One Last Trip into The Matrix," *Film Score Monthly*, 11 November 2003, at http://www.filmscoremonthly.com/articles/2003/11_Nov---Aisle_Seat_One_Last_Trip_Into_The_Matrix.asp (accessed 14 November 2003).

15. Engelhardt and Bond, "Never Ending Style Discourse," online.

16. Randall D. Larson, "Scoring Session: Danny Elfman on *Sleepy Hollow*," *Soundtrack!* Winter 1999/2000, 8.

17. Mauceri, "Music of the Night," online; Chris Cutter and Rudy Koppl, "Onto the Action-Adventure Scoring Battlefield with Danny Elfman: *Spider-Man* and *Men in Black II*," *Soundtrack!* Summer 2002, 17.

18. On *Hulk*, for example, the fact that he was writing the film's second score meant that he only had three days to work on themes before he had to begin scoring. See Jeff Bond, "A Hulking Responsibility," *Film Score Monthly*, June 2003, 23.

19. Clark, "Danny Elfman," online.

20. Randall D. Larson and Ford A. Thaxton, "Scoring Session: Danny Elfman Revisits *Planet of the Apes*," *Soundtrack!* Fall 2001, 4.

21. Greg Pederson, "Danny's Big Adventure: Danny Elfman Embraces the Dark Rites of Film Composition," *Electronic Musician*, February 1997, 106.

22. Larson, "Boingo to *Batman*," 25.

23. Rick Clark, "Danny Elfman," *Mix Magazine*, May 2001, at http://mixonline.com/ar/audio_danny_elfman/ (accessed 24 October 2002).

24. Larson, "*Sleepy Hollow*," 8.

25. Pederson, "Danny's Big Adventure," 104.

26. Schweiger, "Danny Elfman Returns," 18.

27. Engelhardt and Bond, "Never Ending Style Discourse," online.

28. Cooper, *Vertigo*, 30

29. The ultimate Herrmann homage is undoubtedly Elfman's 'recomposition' of Herrmann's score for Gus Van Sant's remake of Hitchcock's *Psycho* in 1998. See also Pederson, "Danny's Big Adventure," 104, for Elfman's discussion of the influence of Herrmann's use of unusual timbres on his own film scoring technique.

30. Adams, "The Evolution of Elfman," *Film Score Monthly*, January 1999, 21.

31. See Schweiger, "Danny Elfman Returns," 20.

32. Alexander Calder (1898–1976) coined the term 'mobile' for his kinetic sculptures, which he also referred to as four-dimensional drawings in that the elements moved in relation to each other, the sculpture changing from moment to moment and therefore existing in the dimension of time as well as three-dimensional space.

Chapter 3

1. Bill Boichel, "Batman: Commodity as Myth," in *The Many Lives of the Batman: Critical Approaches to a Superhero and his Media*, ed. Roberta E. Pearson and William Uricchio (London: BFI; New York: Routledge, 1991), 4

2. Boichel, "Commodity as Myth," 6.

3. Boichel, "Commodity as Myth," 6–7.

4. Will Brooker, *Batman Unmasked: Analyzing a Cultural Icon* (London and New York: Continuum, 2000), 10.

5. Brooker, *Batman Unmasked*, 11, quoting Tony Bennett and Janet Woollacott, *Bond and Beyond* (London: Macmillan, 1987), 20.

6. Brooker, *Batman Unmasked*, 143.

7. For a detailed discussion of this, see Brooker, "Censorship and Queer Readings," chap. 2 in *Batman Unmasked*.

8. Brooker, *Batman Unmasked*, 174.

9. Brooker, *Batman Unmasked*, 53.

10. Bob Kane with Tom Andrae, *Batman and Me* (Forestville, Calif.: Eclipse Books, 1989), 135.

11. Brooker, *Batman Unmasked*, 175. For example, Burton's film makes much of the dualism of Batman and the Joker, and in his 1988 story, Moore "presents Batman and the Joker as distorted mirror images of each other on opposite sides of the law" (Boichel, "Commodity as Myth," 16).

12. This may well have been an intentional production decision, although the shooting script contains at least one scene, unused in the final film, which requires sunlight. However, the overcast skies of the daytime scenes may equally be attributable to the fact that the film was shot in England in the autumn and winter of 1988–1989.

13. The origins of Gotham as a nickname for New York date back to the early nineteenth century and have nothing specific to do with the word 'gothic.' Alluding to a folktale in which the inhabitants of a probably mythical English village of that name pretended to be fools, Washington Irving and others used the name in a series of satirical articles about New York and its inhabitants in the journal *Salmagundi* between 1807 and 1808. See *The American Heritage Dictionary of the English Language*, 4th ed. (Boston: Houghton Mifflin, 2000), s.v. "Gotham."

14. William Uricchio and Roberta E. Pearson, "I'm not fooled by that cheap disguise," in *The Many Lives of the Batman*, 185.

15. Arguably, we have seen this third persona before in the bedroom scene earlier in the film, where Bruce is wearing pajamas. However, it is fairly clear, in context, that it is Bruce who is in bed with Vicki, and that when he leaves the bed to hang upside down from his Bat-frame, he reassumes (or at least, reminds us of) the Batman identity.

16. It is interesting to note a reversal of the usual superhero progression from comic book to television series to film in Joss Whedon's *Buffy the Vampire Slayer*, who has made the journey backward, starting with a film (1992), then becoming a seven-season television series (1997–2003), and then finding a new incarnation in comic-book format as *Fray*.

17. Richard Reynolds, *Superheroes: A Modern Mythology* (London: Batsford, 1992), 12–16.

18. See *Radio Times Guide to Films*, 2000 edition, q.v.

19. Boichel, "Commodity as Myth," 4.

20. Boichel, "Commodity as Myth," 4.

21. Boichel, "Commodity as Myth," 8.

22. Reynolds, *Superheroes*, 67.

23. Superman breaks one of his father's rules by turning back time in order to save Lois's life, but the fact that he acts purely out of love means that his apparent fall from grace is actually a saving grace—it would have been unforgivable for him to fail to save her if he truly loves her.

Chapter 4

1. At the time of its release, *Batman*'s running time was given as 126 minutes, a figure that persists in all the film guides and in the official literature of the film. Both the video and DVD releases, however, have a running time of 121 minutes, although there is no indication of any cuts having been made to the film, including the end credits, prior to its initial video release. However, a curious anomaly of the music is that it consistently sounds almost a semitone sharper than the written score. The 121 minutes running time of the video and DVD represents a 4 percent reduction of the original duration. If, in the process of transferring the film to video in 1989 the film was (inadvertently or otherwise) speeded up by four percent, this would have resulted in all the pitches in the film being raised by approximately three quarters of a semitone, with the result that C would sound like a rather flat C♯, as is indeed the case. This is the only explanation that can be offered for both the difference in running times and the discrepancy between scored and sounded pitches in the written and aural musical texts, although it is surprising, if this is the case, that there is no visible sense of the movement being slightly too fast, and that there are no audible distortions of the soundtrack. The CD recording of the soundtrack, however, sounds at the pitch written, which rather discounts the other possibility that the entire score was, for some reason, transposed up a semitone on the day of the recording. If it is the case that the film has been speeded up, then Elfman wrote seventy-four minutes of music, reduced to seventy-one in the transfer to video.

2. The source of this information is the CDs issued by *Film Score Monthly* on their limited edition Silver Age Classics label which, like the companion Golden Age Classic label, issues complete recordings of film scores, including unused material and alternate versions of cues.

3. Original spellings of titles from the score have been retained in this table, even when these are slightly anomalous.

4. The duration of cues is based on the commercially available recording of the film as issued on video and DVD. As with the observations in note 1 above, these durations are approximately 4 percent shorter than indicated in Elfman's written score.

5. Robert Stam, *Film Theory: An Introduction* (Oxford: Blackwell Press 2001), 221.

6. David Cooper, *Bernard Herrmann's* Vertigo: *A Film Score Handbook* (Westport, Conn.: Greenwood Press, 2001), 36.

7. K. J. Donnelly, "The Classical Film Score Forever? *Batman, Batman Returns* and Post-Classical Film Music," in *Contemporary Hollywood Cinema*, ed. Steve Neale and Murray Smith (London and New York: Routledge, 1998), 150.

8. Donnelly, "Post-Classical Film Music," 150.

9. Robert L. Doerschuk, "Danny Elfman: The Agony and the Ecstasy of Scoring *Batman*," *Keyboard*, October 1989, 18–19.

10. Jeff Bond, "Tale of the Cape," *Film Score Monthly*, January 2000, 28.

11. It is also worth noting that all of the *Indiana Jones* films end with this march rather than beginning with it.

12. R. Serge Denisoff and William D. Romanowski, *Risky Business: Rock in Film* (London and New Brunswick: Transaction, 1991), 693, quoted in Donnelly, "Post-Classical Film Music," 146.

13. See, for example, Randall D. Larson, "Danny Elfman: From Boingo to *Batman*," *Soundtrack!* September 1990, 25; Bob Remstein, "In Control," *New Zealand Film Music Bulletin*, August 1990, 10; Frederick C. Szebin and Steve Biodrowski, "Interview with Danny Elfman," *Soundtrack!* March 1997, 4; Randall D. Larson, "Scoring Session: Danny Elfman on *Sleepy Hollow*," *Soundtrack!* Winter 1999/2000, 8.

14. See also Donnelly, "Post-Classical Film Music," 144–146.

15. Royal S. Brown, *Overtones and Undertones: Reading Film Music* (London and Berkeley: University of California Press, 1994), 266.

16. Anwar Brett, "Dancing with the Devil," *Film Review Special Issue*: The Lost World *and* Batman and Robin, no. 20 (1997), 19.

17. Donnelly, "Post-Classical Film Music," 144.

18. Donnelly, "Post-Classical Film Music," 145.

19. Theodor Adorno and Hanns Eisler, *Composing for the Films* (New York: Oxford University Press, 1947); reprint, with a new introduction by Graham McCann (London: Athelone Press, 1994), 75.

20. 'On-screen' is extended here to mean not only when Bruce-Batman is visible to the audience but when, for example, he is not visible to us but is obviously present in the scene and visible to other characters.

21. Claudia Gorbman, "Aesthetics in the Age of Gump," *Film Score Monthly*, March 1996, 30. It should be pointed out that this is not Gorbman's own opinion but what she perceives to be the opinions of film critics, musicologists, and composers who object to the use of pop songs in film soundtracks.

22. Gorbman, "Aesthetics," 30.

23. Anahid Kassabian, *Hearing Film: Tracking Identifications in Contemporary Hollywood Cinema* (New York and London: Routledge 2001), passim.

24. Jonathan Rosenbaum, "Are We Having Fun?" *Sight and Sound* 59, no. 2 (1990), 96–97.

25. Andrew Ross, "Ballots, Bullets, or Batmen: Can Cultural Studies Do the Right Thing?" *Screen* 31, no. 1 (1990), 31. Ross's italics.

26. Jeff Smith, *The Sounds of Commerce: Marketing Popular Film Music* (New York: Columbia University Press, 1998), 205.

27. Smith, *The Sounds of Commerce*, 189.

28. Smith's own account (*The Sounds of Commerce*, 218–219) of *Robin Hood* implies that he remembers the song occurring within the film narrative rather than in the end credits, while Elfman himself, defending Prince's songs in *Batman*, compares Prince's contribution favorably to what he appears to re-

member as the anachronism of Bryan Adams singing a pop song in medieval England. (See Daniel Schweiger, "Danny Elfman Returns," *Soundtrack!* September 1992, 19.) Perhaps if "Scandalous" had been released as a single before *Batman*, a similar process of mutual promotion and familiarity with the theme might have occurred, but "Scandalous" was never going to be a strong choice as 'the song from the motion picture,' despite its placement in the end credits, the spot usually reserved for that song. "Scandalous" lacks a melodic and easily singable vocal line—it is no coincidence that Elfman uses the accompaniment motif as his love theme, as the vocal line is highly idiosyncratic.

29. Gorbman, "Aesthetics"; Donnelly, "Post-Classical Film Music."

30. Brown, *Overtones and Undertones*; Kathryn Kalinak, *Settling the Score: Music and the Classical Hollywood Film* (London and Madison: University of Wisconsin Press, 1994).

31. Smith, *The Sounds of Commerce*, 238, n. 14.

32. Daniel Schweiger, "Danny Elfman Returns," 19.

33. Schweiger, "Danny Elfman Returns," 19.

34. Smith, *The Sounds of Commerce*, 197.

35. Smith, *The Sounds of Commerce*, 198.

Chapter 5

1. See Kate Daubney, *Max Steiner's* Now, Voyager: *A Film Score Guide* (Westport, Conn.: Greenwood Press, 2000), 15.

2. I am grateful to Dr. David Cooper for this observation about the effect sequencers might have on the notation of the score.

3. This correspondence is held in the Harry Ransom Humanities Research Center, University of Texas at Austin. The necessity of three-act structures for films is widely debated and many great films clearly do not have one (e.g., *2001: A Space Odyssey* has a four-act structure, and many films have what is closer to two acts and a brief epilogue) but the accepted model is that the first and last acts should each occupy between 20 and 30 percent of the film, with the second act being the longest and lasting between 40 to 60 percent of the film's running time. *Batman* is 121 minutes long: its first act is twenty-nine minutes (24 percent) and its last act is thirty-one minutes (26 percent), leaving the second act at sixty-one minutes taking up 50 percent of the film. The typical narrative impetus of a three-act structure is that in act 1, a problem is discovered or created; in act 2, the hero attempts to solve the problem but usually makes it worse; and in act 3, he finally manages to solve it, usually in the nick of time. This also corresponds to a romantic scenario of 'meet the girl, lose the girl, marry the girl,' and both of these plotlines are evident in *Batman*'s act structure, the 'problem' scenario being that of Batman and the Joker and the 'romantic' scenario Bruce and Vicki.

4. See Sam Hamm, "Batman," screenplay, first draft, 1986, at http://www.dailyscript.com/scripts/batman_early.html (accessed 7 August 2002).

5. At fifty-six pages, this is one of the longest sections of the score, and one of several orchestrated not by Bartek but by Steven Scott Smalley, who does not appear in the film's end credits. Although it became widely known following Elfman's *Keyboard* interview that Shirley Walker had leant a hand with the orchestration, Smalley's orchestration of some of the longer cues (e.g., "Joker's Commercial" and "Waltz") has remained uncredited. Apart from the fact that Smalley's handwriting is a good deal more legible, the scoring of this cue in terms of the balance of instruments and the roles they play is itself good evidence of the level of detail in Elfman's short scores, as there is no discernable difference in the final sound and style of the orchestration when compared to Bartek's.

6. Charles Rosen, *Schoenberg* (Glasgow: Fontana, 1976), 55.

7. See chapter 4, n. 25.

8. The horn appears to have been a late addition to this cue: as is seen in several other cues, changes have been made on Bartek's score using a different pen, and here the original intention appears to have been to have just violin and harp carrying the melody, with the oboe and horn added later.

9. Ian Garwood, "Must You Remember This? Orchestrating the 'Standard' Pop Song in *Sleepless in Seattle*," in *Movie Music: The Film Reader*, ed. Kay Dickinson (London and New York: Routledge, 2003), 109.

Chapter 6

1. For those with perfect pitch, it should be pointed out that all musical examples and references to key are based on the written score. What appears to be a slight acceleration of the film's running time produces a sharpening of pitches throughout, with the result that C, for example, sounds as a slightly flat C♯. See chapter 4, n. 1.

2. Giorgio Biancorosso, "Beginning Credits and Beyond: Music and the Cinematic Imagination," in *Echo: A Music-Centered Journal* 3 (Spring 2001), at http://www.echo.ucla.edu (accessed 5 June 2003).

3. It is clear from the score that the main title was originally intended to be considerably longer than the eighty-five bars, lasting two-and-a-half minutes, which appear in the film. Not only is it subtitled "Short version," but an addendum sheet from the discarded long version shows the end of the main title cue at bar 131, which would bring the cue to almost four minutes duration.

4. On the CD recording, this happens at one minute, twenty seconds. On the DVD, this moment occurs between the on-screen credits for Jack Palance and Marion Dougherty.

5. On the CD recording, this happens at one minute, fourteen seconds. On the DVD, this moment coincides with the credit for Jack Palance.

6. On the CD recording, this happens at one minute, forty seconds. On the DVD, this moment occurs halfway through the credit for Chris Kenny.

7. On the CD recording, this happens at two minutes, twelve seconds. On the DVD, this moment occurs just before the end of the credit for Prince.

8. There is another very specific reference to Batman's connection to vampires in the name of one of the principal villains of *Batman Returns*, where Max Schreck (Christopher Walken) is named after the actor who played cinema's original vampire in *Nosferatu* (1922).

9. The two bars here are actually in 6/4 and 7/4.

10. Elfman has said in an interview that this was the first time he had used a choir in a film score (see Mark Russell and James Young, *Screencraft: Film Music* [Crans-Près-Céligny: RotoVision, 2000], 156) although this is not actually true: he had previously used a choir in the main titles of both *Scrooged* and *Beetlejuice* in 1988. It may, however, be the first time he used a choir within the main body of a film rather than in a main title or end credit cue.

11. Elfman acknowledged the allusion in an online interview. See "AOL Interview with Danny Elfman," May 1995, at http://www.boingo.org/articles/aol.html (accessed 1 November 2002).

12. The *Dies Irae* is found, for example, in the main title cues of Kubrick's *The Shining* (1986) and Marco Brambilla's *Demolition Man* (1993). See also William H. Rosar, "The *Dies Irae* in *Citizen Kane*: Musical Hermeneutics Applied To Film Music," in *Film Music: Critical Approaches*, ed. K. J. Donnelly (Edinburgh: Edinburgh University Press, 2001), 103–116.

13. The connection between Barber's *Adagio* and mourning was reinforced more recently when it was used during the memorial service for the victims of the World Trade Center attack of 11 September 2001 in New York.

14. There was a brief, *pianissimo* cue written for this scene entitled "Joker Flies to Gotham," but the sheer level of volume produced by the exploding factory, helicopter engines, and the Joker's megaphone are probably the main reasons why it was unused.

Bibliography

Adams, Doug. "Tales from the Black Side: An Interview with Danny Elfman." *Film Score Monthly*, June 1997: 20–26.

———. "The Evolution of Elfman." *Film Score Monthly*, January 1999: 20–23, 46.

Adorno, Theodor and Hanns Eisler. *Composing for the Films*. New York: Oxford University Press, 1947. Reprint, with a new introduction by Graham Mc-Cann, London: Athelone Press, 1994.

Batman [motion picture]. 1989. United States: Warner Bros.

Batman Returns [motion picture]. 1992. United States: Warner Bros.

Beetlejuice [motion picture]. 1988. United States: Warner Bros.

Bettencourt, Scott. *"Film Score Monthly*'s Top Forty Hit Makers." *Film Score Monthly*, September 2002: 18–29.

Biancorosso, Giorgio. "Beginning Credits and Beyond: Music and the Cinematic Imagination." *Echo: A Music-Centered Journal* 3 (Spring 2001). At www. echo.ucla.edu (accessed 5 June 2003).

Big Fish [motion picture]. 2003. United States: Columbia Pictures.

Boichel, Bill. "Batman: Commodity as Myth." In *The Many Lives of the Batman: Critical Approaches to a Superhero and his Media*, edited by Roberta E. Pearson and William Uricchio, 4–17. London: BFI; New York: Routledge, 1991.

Bond, Jeff. "Tale of the Cape." *Film Score Monthly*, January 2000: 27–31.

———. "A Whole Different Animal." *Film Score Monthly*, July 2001: 24–28.

———. "A Hulking Responsibility." *Film Score Monthly*, June 2003: 22–24.

Brett, Anwar. "Dancing with the Devil." *Film Review Special Issue*: The Lost World *and* Batman and Robin, no. 20 (1997): 16–19.

Brooker, Will. *Batman Unmasked: Analyzing a Cultural Icon*. London and New York: Continuum, 2000.

Brown, Royal S. *Overtones and Undertones: Reading Film Music*. London and Berkeley: University of California Press, 1994.

Burlingame, Jon. "Danny Elfman on the Move." *Soundtrack!* September 1990: 21.

Clark, Rick. "Danny Elfman." *Mix Magazine*, 1 May 2001. At http://mixonline. com/ar/audio_danny_elfman/ (accessed 24 October 2002).

Cooper, David. *Bernard Herrmann's* Vertigo: *A Film Score Handbook*. Westport, Conn.: Greenwood Press, 2001.

Darling, Cary. "Only Eight Lads: Boingo's Difficult Teenage Years." *Bay Area Music Magazine*, 8 May 1987: 24–28.

Davis, Richard. *Complete Guide to Film Scoring: The Art and Business of Writing Music for Movies and Television*. Boston, Mass.: Berklee Press, 1999.

Daubney, Kate. *Max Steiner's* Now, Voyager: *A Film Score Guide*. Westport, Conn.: Greenwood Press, 2000.

Deutsch, Didier. "Danny Elfman Interview." *Soundtrack!* December 1993: 8–9.

Doerschuk, Robert L. "Danny Elfman: The Agony and the Ecstasy of Scoring *Batman*." *Keyboard*, October 1989: 83–95.

Dolores Claiborne [motion picture]. 1995. United States: Columbia Pictures.

Donnelly, K. J. "*Batman, Batman Returns* and Post-Classical Film Music." In *Contemporary Hollywood Cinema*, edited by Steve Neale and Murray Smith, 142–155. London and New York: Routledge, 1998.

———, ed. *Film Music: Critical Approaches*. Edinburgh: Edinburgh University Press, 2001.

Dursin, Andy. "One Last Trip into The Matrix." *Film Score Monthly*, 11 November 2003. At http://www.filmscoremonthly.com/articles/2003/11_Nov---Aisle_Seat_One_Last_Trip_Into_The_Matrix.asp (accessed 14 November 2003)

Edward Scissorhands [motion picture]. 1990. United States: Twentieth Century Fox.

Elfman, Danny. "Batman." Score. 1989. Warner Bros. Music Library. Los Angeles.

———. "An Open Letter from Danny Elfman." *Keyboard*, March 1990: 47, 62, 64.

———. *Batman Returns: Music from the Motion Picture*. Warner Bros. compact disc 7599-26972-2.

———. *Music for a Darkened Theater: Film and Television Music*. Vol. 2. MCA Records compact disc MCAD2-11550.

———. "Chimp Symphony op. 37." *Planet of The Apes*. Directed by Tim Burton. 114 minutes. Twentieth Century Fox Home Entertainment, 2002. DVD.

Engelhardt, Bill and Jeff Bond. "The Never Ending Style Discourse." *Film Score Monthly*, 27 August, 1997. At http://www.filmscoremonthly.com/articles/1997/27_Aug---Style_discourse.asp (accessed 1 May 2003).

Flans, Robyn. "Oingo Boingo: Mondo Schizo." *Bay Area Music Magazine*, 7 October 1983: 16–19.

Flinn, Caryl. *Strains of Utopia: Gender, Nostalgia and Hollywood Film Music*. Princeton: Princeton University Press, 1992.

Frith, Simon. *Performing Rites: Evaluating Popular Music*. Paperback ed.

Oxford and New York: Oxford University Press, 1998.

Garwood, Ian. "Must You Remember This? Orchestrating the 'Standard' Pop Song in *Sleepless in Seattle*." In *Movie Music: The Film Reader,* edited by Kay Dickinson, 109–117. London and New York: Routledge, 2003.

Glionna, John M. "A Different Beat." *Los Angeles Times Magazine*, 18 April, 1999: 10.

Good Will Hunting [motion picture]. 1997. United States: Miramax Films.

Gorbman, Claudia. "Aesthetics in the Age of Gump." *Film Score Monthly*, March 1996: 30–31.

———. *Unheard Melodies: Narrative Film Music.* Bloomington: Indiana University Press; London: BFI, 1987.

Green, Lucy. *How Popular Musicians Learn: A Way Ahead for Music Education.* Aldershot: Ashgate, 2001.

Hamm, Sam. "Batman." Screenplay, first draft. 1986. At http://www.dailyscript.com/scripts/batman_early.html (accessed 7 August 2002).

Hamm, Sam and Warren Skaaren. "Batman." Screenplay, fifth draft. 1989. At http://www.dailyscript.com/scripts/batman_production.html (accessed 7 August 2002).

Hanke, Ken. "Tim Burton." Parts 1 and 2. *Films in Review* 43 (1992): 374–381; 44 (1993): 40–48.

Hassler-Forest, Dan. "The *Auteur* as Marketing Concept." *Tim Burton: Auteur or Marketing Concept? A Hypertext,* n.d. At www.euronet.nl/users/mcbeijer/dan/home_burton.html (accessed 12 December 2001).

Howe, Desson. "*Batman.*" *The Washington Post*, 23 July 1989. At http://www.washingtonpost.com/wp-srv/style/longterm/movies/videos/batmanpg13howe_a0b220.htm (accessed 20 October 2003).

Hughes, David. *Comic Book Movies.* London: Virgin Books, 2003.

Jackson, Blair. "Oingo Boingo: The Band that Wouldn't Die." *Bay Area Music Magazine*, 5 December 1980: 28–30.

Kalinak, Kathryn. *Settling the Score: Music and the Classical Hollywood Film.* London and Madison: University of Wisconsin Press, 1994.

Kane, Bob with Tom Andrae. *Batman and Me.* Forestville, Calif.: Eclipse Books, 1989.

Kassabian, Anahid. *Hearing Film: Tracking Identifications in Contemporary Hollywood Cinema.* New York and London: Routledge, 2001.

Kendall, Lukas. "Danny Elfman: From *Pee-Wee* to *Batman* to Two Films a Year." Parts 1 and 2. *Film Score Monthly*, October 1995: 13–14; December 1995: 11–14.

———. "Interview: Steve Bartek." *Film Score Monthly*, December 1995: 14–16.

Koppl, Rudy and Chris Cutter. "Onto the Action-Adventure Scoring Battlefield with Danny Elfman: *Spider-Man* and *Men in Black II*." *Soundtrack!* Summer 2002: 12–19.

Kuhn, Annette, ed. *Alien Zone: Cultural Theory and Contemporary Science Fiction Cinema.* London and New York: Verso, 1990.

Lapedis, Hilary. "Popping the Question: The Function and Effect of Popular Music in Cinema." *Popular Music Journal* 18, no. 3 (1999): 367–379.

Larson, Randall D. "Film Music: Danny Elfman, Director Tim Burton's Rock Music Man." *Cinéfantastique*, November 1989: 109, 120.

———. "Danny Elfman: From Boingo to *Batman*." *Soundtrack!* September 1990: 20, 22–27.

———. "Danny Elfman: Expecting the Impossible—Scoring *Mission: Impossible #1*." *Soundtrack!* Summer 2000: 36–37.

———. "Scoring Session: Danny Elfman on *Sleepy Hollow*." *Soundtrack!* Winter 1999/2000: 8–10.

Larson, Randall D. and Ford A. Thaxton. "Scoring Session: Danny Elfman Revisits *Planet of the Apes*." *Soundtrack!* Fall 2001: 4–6.

Lauliac, Christian. "Musique de Film: Danny Elfman." *Positif,* October 1998: 98.

Lowman, Rob. "The Elfman Cometh." *News Dot Com*, 5 August 2001. At http://www.angelfire.com/trek/ortreat/a15.html (accessed 24 October 2002).

Mars Attacks! [motion picture]. 1996. United States: Warner Bros.

Mauceri, Joseph B. "Music of the Night: An Interview with Danny Elfman." *Fear Magazine*, July 1990. At http://www.geocities.com/boingo20001/fear90.html (accessed 20 October 2002).

Mundy, John. *Popular Music on Screen: From Hollywood Musical to Music Video.* Manchester: Manchester University Press, 1999.

Nightmare Before Christmas, The [animation]. 1993. United States: Touchstone Pictures.

Pearson, Roberta E. and William Ulricchio, eds. *The Many Lives of the Batman: Critical Approaches to a Superhero and his Media.* London: BFI; New York: Routledge, 1991.

Pederson, Greg. "Danny's Big Adventure: Danny Elfman Embraces the Dark Rites of Film Composition." *Electronic Musician*, February 1997: 100–108.

Pee-Wee's Big Adventure [motion picture]. 1985. United States: Warner Bros.

Place, Paul. "Danny Elfman: *Planet of the Apes*." *Music from the Movies*, May 2002: 62.

———. "Danny Elfman: *Spider-Man*." *Music from the Movies*, July/August 2002: 52.

Planet of the Apes [motion picture]. 2001. United States: Twentieth Century Fox.

Remstein, Bob. "In Control." *New Zealand Film Music Bulletin*, August 1990: 9–11.

Reynolds, Richard. *Superheroes: A Modern Mythology.* London: Batsford, 1992.

Rosar, William H. "The *Dies Irae* in *Citizen Kane*: Musical Hermeneutics Applied to Film Music." In *Film Music: Critical Approaches*, edited by K. J. Donnelly, 103–116. Edinburgh: Edinburgh University Press, 2001.

Rosen, Charles. *Schoenberg*. Glasgow: Fontana, 1976.

Rosenbaum, Jonathan. "Are We Having Fun?" *Sight and Sound* 59, no. 2 (1990): 96–97.

Ross, Andrew. "Ballots, Bullets, or Batmen: Can Cultural Studies Do the Right Thing?" *Screen* 31, no. 1 (1990): 26–44.

Rubin, Rosina. "Composer Danny Elfman." *Premiere*, January 1991: 42.

Russell, Mark and James Young. *Screencraft: Film Music*. Crans-Près-Céligny: RotoVision, 2000.

Rynning, Roald. "Danny Elfman—Composer." *Empire*, August 1991: 34.

Schweiger, Daniel. "Danny Elfman Returns." *Soundtrack!* September 1992: 17–20.

Sleepy Hollow [motion picture]. 1999. United States: Paramount.

Smith, Jeff. *The Sounds of Commerce: Marketing Popular Film Music*. New York: Columbia University Press, 1998.

Smith, Jeff and J. Clive Matthews. *Tim Burton*. London: Virgin Film, 2002.

Sommersby [motion picture]. 1993. United States: Warner Bros.

Stam, Robert. *Film Theory: An Introduction*. Oxford: Blackwell Press, 2001.

Szebin, Frederick C. and Steve Biodrowski. "Martian Music: Composer Danny Elfman on Burtonizing the Golden Sci-Fi Scores of the Past." *Cinéfantastique*, January 1997: 28–29.

———. "Interview with Danny Elfman." *Soundtrack!* March 1997: 4–7.

Thomas, Philip. "The Misfit." *Empire*, August 1991: 54–58.

Uricchio, William and Roberta E. Pearson. "I'm Not Fooled by that Cheap Disguise." In *The Many Lives of the Batman: Critical Approaches to a Superhero and his Media*, edited by Roberta E. Pearson and William Uricchio, 182–213. London: BFI; New York: Routledge, 1991.

Willman, Christopher. "Twentieth Century Schizoid Man." *Grammy Magazine*, Summer 1994: 20–25.

Zollo, Paul. "Danny Elfman: Upholding Tradition (with a Sense of Humor)." *The Hollywood Reporter: Film and TV Music Special Report*, January 1989: S-57–59.

Additional Web Resources

Boingo 2000 at http://www.geocities.com/boingo20001
Beyond Insanity at http://www.angelfire.com/trek/ortreat
Celluloid Tunes as http://www.celluloidtunes.com
Dan's Boingo Page at http://www.boingo.org
Music for a Darkened People at http://elfman.filmmusic.com

Index

About the Author

Janet K. Halfyard is a senior lecturer at Birmingham Conservatoire, a faculty of the University of Central England, where she teaches courses in film music, and twentieth-century music history and performance practice. She is also active as a performer of contemporary vocal music. Her publications include papers on extended vocal technique and film and television music, particularly on music in the television series *Buffy the Vampire Slayer* and *Angel*.